F I C T I O N

WHEN CALIFORNIA
WAS AN ISLAND   Barbara Haas   1987

P O E T R Y

POEMS: SELECTED & NEW   Tony Curtis   1986

THE ADVENTURE   Frederick Pollack   1986

THE DOUBLE GENESIS   Dennis Sampson   1985

BACKTRACKING   Vern Rutsala   1985

S T O R Y   L I N E   P R E S S

When California Was an Island

STORIES by BARBARA HAAS

THIS SERIES IS MADE POSSIBLE BY THE GENEROUS SUPPORT
of the
NICHOLAS ROERICH MUSEUM, NEW YORK

•

ISBN: 0-934257-10-8 (paper)
ISBN: 0-934257-11-6 (cloth)

•

Published by Story Line Press
A subsidiary of The Reaper, Inc.
325 Ocean View Avenue
Santa Cruz, California 95062

•

Book Design by Lysa Howard – McDowell
Typesetting by The Type Factory

ACKNOWLEDGEMENTS

STORIES PREVIOUSLY APPEARING IN THESE CREDITED MAGAZINES:

LIKE A CACTUS IN A FIELD OF CORN .... The Western Humanities Review

ON MU .... The Denver Quarterly

DYING IN THE GOLDENWEST .... The Virginia Quarterly Review

(First appeared as) C.A.'s ADVICE .... The Reaper

PRINCESS GILDA TALKS TO THE UNBORN ..... Pulpsmith

WHEN CALIFORNIA WAS AN ISLAND .... The Hudson Review

for George

TABLE OF CONTENTS

A Wolf in the Heart...................................1

Like a Cactus in a Field of Corn 19

On Mu..37

Dying in the Goldenwest.......................53

The Green Life 67

You'll Remember Me Long After.................91

Princess Gilda Talks to the Unborn...........109

When California Was an Island 123

A place belongs forever to whoever claims it hardest, remembers it most obsessively, wrenches it from itself, shapes it, renders it, loves it so radically that he remakes it in his image ...

Joan Didion

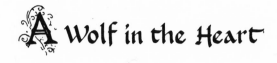

A Wolf in the Heart

Using no spades or rakes, the men took turns operating a small yellow tractor whose shovel brought up huge bites of the earth every time. Within minutes, a pyramid of dirt had grown to a man's height and one newly opened grave had formed. Over it, they labored to erect a canopy of gorgeously striped canvas on four poles; its ends flapped in the breeze, made a snapping noise, but the poles—rooted more firmly than slender trees—did not sway. Then, as the men hopped back on to the tractor and rode off across the hills in the opposite direction, the grave lay there, a sky of orange, blue, and purple bars ballooning above it, the dirt around its edges drying in the air.

Chas and Hazel sat not 100 yards away, buried in conversation. "Oh, wow," he was saying, *"love,"* as if she'd offered to him hidden among crackers and breadsticks and potato chips some exquisite morsel. She watched him take it up; he sampled it. And savoring the words, allowing them to roll across his tongue, he said, "Annette and I love." He arched his eyebrows in pleasant surprise at the doubt which must have crossed her face. "We do!"

Exercising a boldness to which Hazel felt more than entitled—for it was *her* food they were eating, *her* granny quilt on which they now sat, *her* picnic basket atop which he'd propped his feet, *her* box of chocolates from which he did from time to time lift some rarity; and the view? well, she had herself chosen it—in that atmosphere of boldness she allowed her thought to form. *"You* love? Well, not so much that anyone'd notice."

"Annette and I are intimate. We are! But we are for reasons that are a little off the beaten path." He had a bite of a carrot stick. "It's enough to know that in some other world, certified, unfaked, 24 karat intimacy might be possible. You know? All wool and a yard wide?"

" 'Wool'? "

His shrug came quick, his smile lopsidedly. "The kind of card-carrying intimacy you imagine your mother and father had."

With that, she gazed out toward the horizon, past all the headstones and statuary gleaming in the sun. Pinelawn was the only pocket of tranquility in all of Orange County, a place where the throng, the multitide, the hoards, were all *below* ground, not *above* and actively competing. Though beautiful, it no longer had uniform rows striping its hills; time and a slight erosion had wrinkled them. Her eyes roamed freely from the stone tips of angel's wings to the cherubs and lambs

and icons of red granite—and then down to that flat, mani-
cured area near the chain link fence whose graves, like all the
other graves, had bushy green wreaths stuck on stilty, birdlike
legs in the ground. Would she mind lying there for all eter-
nity? Dead, would it really matter? The entire place struck her
as something serving not the dearly departed so much as
those who remained. Like her and Chas, lunching amid it.
Tiny reflective ponds glittered out at her from the sides of
hills like jewels clasped by the earth; tall stands of evergreen
cast their cool darkness across the grass. It was all so restive
she scarcely felt a pulse.

After a bit Hazel became aware of Chas spreading soft
cheese on a cracker. "You 'love' Annette because you can't
always 'love' Darby," she said.

He said that that was true.

"Your first choice would be *Darby*, not Annette, were she
not—well, you know, not the way we know Darby to be?"

He told her she had it all.

Hazel leaned forward so quickly she unsettled the box of
chocolates; several fluted paper cups fluttered across the lawn.
"You've both been passed over. *That's* what unites you."

Chas stuck his hand up between them. "Look, when we're
in each other's arms, we are indistinguishable from the peo-
ple who are falling in love and those who already have.
Fallen, you know."

"You're saying you *look* like *them*. Is that it?" She helped
him along this, the least familiar stretch of their oh-so-
familiar terrain. "Like dress-up on Halloween?"

He was a step ahead of her. "This isn't the basis of a long,
comfortable *anything*. It's like making a meal from Happy
Hour hors d'oeuvres. Or drinking a glass of beer that's all
foam. Is it a feast within a famine? Well, it's still—it's still
...It's something. I mean, aren't *you* ever hungry?"

There was an added heat to the way he said this, and she
had to stop for a moment to try to see things the way he
wanted her to. A plate of spinach dip, nachos, and mozzarella
marinara floated up from somewhere. Hopeless! "So when
you're together you're thinking of Darby and she's thinking
of—well, whoever she's thinking of." When he only smiled
somewhat sadly at the picture she'd painted, she fell back
against the quilt, rummaging through the small tools of her
mind, searching through her rulers, her compasses and calip-
ers for just the instrument that would measure the dimension
of what he'd given form. After a bit she lifted her own trium-
phant gaze to his face; he met her there. "But that's not loving."

His shrug tossed it back at her. "That's not?"

The longer her eyes remained locked with his, the more she began to see not them, but *into* them, *beyond* them, to what he saw. The image took shape; it mesmerized her; her voice came in a kind of halting murmur. "But it doesn't have to be." More than the words, something seemed to pass between them—a sticky spider's web of understanding spun so fine it was a white mist; it joined their limbs, sagged in the air like a cloud. She felt, barely perceptibly, its tug. "But doesn't it?" she asked at last. "I mean have to be. Loving, you know." The red paper heart with the wide border of intricate white lace lay on the picnic hamper between them, and when she lifted it, the effect was as if she had taken up a scythe and slashed through what joined them. "Yesterday *was* Valentine's Day, after all. Didn't you want to celebrate love?"

He appeared wounded. "Love," he breathed. And in the place where, on other occasions, a fiery argument might begin he only sighed, holding her gaze for what seemed as long as he could before tearing away to look past her. She turned to look, too. There stood a cluster of firs. A battalion of ribboned wreaths and other greenery. White dots of graves lay sprinkled across the hills. She knew he saw not those things but the scene he had fixed in his mind's eye, as if an eidetic image. He'd seen it all, when he stopped by her place to pick her up. He'd seen everything from the night before stationed about her living room with all the importance of sacred relics in a shrine: a champagne cork on the counter; two steak bones rapidly petrifying in the corner where her dog, Bof, had been worrying them; a hardened puddle of pink candlewax, one half-burnt cone of patchouli incense; roses Troy had brought her, long-stemmed red ones, for on Love's day he believed in going strictly by the book. And the things they suggested, there though not visible: the feeling in her belly as her body digested its good meal, and the feeling, still lower, the remembered feel of Troy inside: noises they'd made, the wet sounds of their bodies, the music played, the bubble bath taken, the scented body oil rubbed. Now Chas' gaze roamed from that distance back to the quilt and then slowly across her body to fix itself however briefly on her left hand and the ring which in the sun shot color around like crystals do.

These were the aftereffects of her love; these were its humble remains.

"Forgive me," he said. He was shaking his head, staring down at his hands which were joined between his knees before him. "I don't mean to hang crape." The slump of his shoulders showed her how unimpressed he was with what he saw.

Her gaze fell, as if with a life and will of its own, to his groin—remaining there for several moments—then ascending to his mouth, the remembered blush and fullness of his lips replaced with a tension which seemed to draw a fine, colorless line, like a crease, across them.

"Well, *I* love you, Chas," she said. Hazel rubbed the bottoms of her feet against the soles of his. It was the only surface of their skin that had, since coming together that morning, touched—and even then it wasn't skin: both still had their nubby socks on.

II

But she refused to apologize for love's earthly remains!

This thought stirred, seemed to rise up through heat waves and shimmer there in the distance, right on the edge of the world. She peered from thickly lidded eyes—she and Chas having finished their lunch and now lain down to nap—as if to see the thought, panting there. At first she'd sensed a true prescence, like a lone figure wandering about the periphery of the Garden of Resurrection. At first she'd opened her eyes, scanning the distance for that figure, the specter of a man, his hat wedged down tightly over his brow, a cigarette slanting from his lips and the wreath of smoke which would hang like a mist in the stillness. Barely on the horizon, not moving any closer, neither insinuating itself in any way nor bristling with the need to be recognized—all of which made *her* bristle —the figure seemed to keep sentry. It wove a path amid the statuary, threaded its way in and among the tombstones, seemed to bind all the deaths each to the other, as if with silken twine from the same garment. She had more than once awakened at the very blackest hour of the night, when poor fortune is distorted even more absurdly out of proportion than fear can naturally do. This was daylight's equivalent— but with a difference: glimpsed through the paralysis of afternoon sleep, a thing seems radiant with its own life. For several moments her gaze walked the horizon, expecting to meet the radiance, that rambling disinterested soul in whom she believed, until it quite naturally stumbled upon that bare, dark oblong—a grave the workmen had earlier opened.

What was to suppress the urge to go over and look in it, and then, standing over it, the urge to spit, or to leap into it, someone else's final resting place, never meant for her? Not Chas who lay on the quilt several granny squares away, suspended in his own paralysis as in aspic, a little dribble of saliva forming at the corner of his mouth, looking very much as he must at Annette's when he sleeps the sleep of the unloved. Such a contrast to the way she lay in Troy's arms after making a love that could abandon her atop some high, rare summit to slide down its steep sides! Hazel imagined an expression of the purest tranquility, as if chiseled upon her features, just after. A thing with which one didn't argue.

More than once, however, she and *Chas* had argued about the way he conducted his romance; more than once their arguments had ended unsatisfactorily with her pulling rank on him, poising as she did atop Love as if it were a mountain for which she alone—well-courted, long-engaged, and now married—had endured the agony to climb.

That last had occurred a couple months before, during the tempestuous weather of December, as they'd strolled along Balboa. In any other season, in another place, she'd expect to see some raging electrical storm blow in—but at that time of year the clouds didn't move, only hung low over the Pacific, shrouding ships, sailboats, and surfers in a pewter-colored vapor. And the water hit shore not in waves, but came rolling forth in thick, excruciatingly slow swells, like syrup. Where sunbathers had lain in summer was now overcovered with a dense jungle of kelp and ocean debris: tar, wood smoothed beyond its natural properties, plastic, more weeds. Choked with sea grass and sand, the waves had languished there, as if they had not the energy to rush back out, barely seeping back to sea when they did go. She and Chas had followed, that day, where their shadows led, the sun at their backs casting the blurred forms—unmistakably human—across the sand before them. Eight feet tall, she thought, and then, correcting herself, Or *long*—because the shadows appeared to hover over the sand. Seemed to crawl across the sand like smoke.

Sweat had trickled down the side of her face from her hairline as she walked. She was just a woman kicking through the sand, the man beside her frequently stooping to pick up a garland of kelp and wave it in the December light like a banner. But a frustration had quietly raged underneath it all as she strolled along, occasionally squinting up into the sun. Chas was telling her his dream of the night before, and she was listening as if forcibly restrained. *It* had set her off—because he didn't see the dream as a mirror to the subconscious self, but as a prophesy, something which portended great things—whether tragic or not—to come. "I'm lying in bed, looking out the window, and there, riding steadily on the wind, is a kite made of bedsheets. It's fabulous! Instead of having another bedsheet for the tail, it has a man and a woman who cling to the fabric and twine around each other. All at once a gust of wind lifts the kite up, 100 feet. It rises straight up, like on an elevator. The tail whips and snaps in the air, their bodies undulate. *Her* hair flows and ripples from her skull like a flag made of golden thread. It's the most thrilling thing in the world! And then the man falls off." Chas scooped the air with his hand. "He plummets. When they find him, his pelvis is buried five inches in the ground. From the impact." And then he added, unnecessarily, but his voice nevertheless thick with its own meaning, "He wasn't able to hold on anymore."

Having stopped near some pilings while he finished telling the dream, they had then continued across the beach.

"I tell you, it *scares* me. What it means."

She didn't ask what he assumed it meant.

"You know?" he said. "Aren't dreams spooky?"

He had his superstitions, ones in which she didn't share. That's why she kept quiet; *he* kept them alive. He liked to think if his palm itched it meant money, and if his ears burned it meant good gossip he'd soon learn. Once, months before, she had waited in his apartment, listening to wire hangers clink together in his closet, as he dressed. When he had wandered back out into the living room, he was still buttoning his shirt. He showed her how a corner of his shirt-tail was folded up and turned inside out, like a fragile ear, and explained to her what this meant.

"I'll get new clothing soon—like within the week—but only, *only*, if I kiss this before turning it right side out."

She'd touched the fold, half expecting it to emit an electrical charge. "Is it a passionate kiss, or is it like kissing your sister?"

He grinned. "Depends on what kind of new garment you want." Then he brought the fabric to his lips; his tongue darted out experimentally. Hazel had not seen the new garment—but she imagined Annette had, or Darby, who knows? Perhaps both.

Now, Chas twirled a length of kelp above his head like a lasso and then flung it into a retreating wave. "I hate to think of what it all means. For me and Darby. We're together, then we're not. We're together, then we're not. She's jerking me around like a kite on the wind. I tell you, that woman's going to be the death of me. *She* sent me that dream, that *night*mare!"

The thing was, his misery loved company. When he talked to her like this, she thought really he was saying, "Come. Join me." And despite the anger balled up inside, she found herself eventually giving in, going along, unravelling, joining in—her misery, after all, in love with company, too. Was this ground they, mutually, never tired of travelling? A road map which perennially shaped and perfected itself? "You and Darby have talked about why she's unfaithful, and she says it hasn't solely to do with pleasure."

He vigorously assented. "She says it has to do with her poor self-image. That she sometimes" —here he swallowed— "hates herself afterward."

" But she does it anyway."

He could only nod and even then just barely. "The only rule for our relationship is that we can date people just as long as..."

"...as long as the other doesn't find out." It was all so rote! This the part of the map, the stretch of road that, as other people, a sister and brother, have blood in common, she and Chas could share. "But you've known every time."

"I've known every time it's happened."

"As she has known about you and Annette."

He shrugged. "Well, she's a sensitive woman."

"And there's jealousy between you."

His inhalation sounded over the ocean noise; the breath swelled in his chest, he held it, waiting as if for a wave to peak and break before expiring. "There's everything between us."

"So, why prolong it?"

At that he passed his hands before him, the fingers seeming to catch in many sticky and immeasurably dense threads. The gesture was a dead ringer for the way a musician might pluck tacky harp strings. For a long minute they both stood in silence, as if what he would say were stuck fast in the imagined webbing. When his eyes locked with hers, Hazel inclined her head to one side, in the attitude of patiently waiting saints, as if to lift him with her gaze alone.

Wasn't this their exit? The paved road which became a gravel one, then turned into a dirt road and wound in upon itself until it finally got lost in the dense distorted dark of a forest? Could he be coaxed to wander with her deep into weeds, far from what was known, to a destination at which even she could only guess? Did her question and, standing before him now, her attitude tempt him toward dangerous terrain, drawing him nearer, as she hoped, to the Truth as she saw it, the Truth resting—as if buoyed up on a sofa, its legs crossed and with tea cup in hand—on the fact that this was not love, that he didn't know love, that he dwelled in loveless misery? Because wasn't love having togetherness? And things shared? And mutual respect and a retention of dignity? Wasn't *that* the love she understood and could leisurely sip as if it were yet one more bottle she'd brought up from the cellar of fine wines to which she had private and unlimited access? Or was it something else, a forest so deep, a jungle so dark, vegetation so dense as never to be cut, a land of sharp bamboo edges, parasites that feed on the host, eventually killing it, vines that overtake you and in which you can only stumble and pitch about, as in choking, clutching kudzu?

His eyes gave nothing.

At any other time during their friendship she could foresee their immediate future, could calculate the depth of it, the length, the dimension of it, as if it were as real as a slab of something laid out on a table before her; not so now. His hesitation, his silence, held her absolutely suspended. It was as though, having hoisted *her* up, *he'd* managed to dangle her—above teeming, spiked peril—by a thread that had drawn taut to snapping

"Why do I prolong it?" Chas wondered aloud. "I prolong it because . . . "—and here she could only twirl about, waiting, at the end of that from which he'd hung her—"well, I'm in love." It was the way that anyone else might, when asked to scale some awesome precipice, decline, explaining , "Well, I'm a quadroplegiac."

Did she fall?

Didn't she always?

Because that answer, the thing which—in asking—she'd forgotten, had always towered above her. It was a milestone on their map—a national monument, a landmark! But by what optical illusion, if the road toward it were as familiar and tired as all the other ones they travelled, could the way each time seem new? How could she see and not see? For it was clear from their other confrontations that he stuck as fast to his notion of love as the barnacles she now saw stuck fast to pier pilings at the water's edge. Clearer still, in the circularity of their arguing, was her awareness that he could no more be budged from his notions than that crustacean might be displaced by the flick of a finger. Clearest yet of all was the fact that her efforts to unfasten, in him, what evidently had been fastened tight, failed; it was as if the scraped fingers picking at the wet, encrusted wood might never learn. For Chas strolled beside her now as secure in the love he professed as if petrified in it.

Something ignited just beneath her skin. *What*, in coupling with Annette, did he *make?* She meant besides a love that, as if congenitally handicapped, lurched and staggered between them. "For Christ's sake," she cried, "those women use you!"

"No," he said. "No. When you say *that*, I see, truly, how much you can't—won't—understand."

She stopped in the sand with such abruptness it seemed her feet had hotly refused to carry her further. So this was the place to which their shadows had led them—as if an insidious 'X' had marked the spot. Not the ends of the earth, certainly, but it would, for her and Chas, suffice on that day: if she dug straight down she'd uncover not China but sea serpents and dragons and mayhem buried there. "What distinguishes your love from your pain? What right do you have to use that word? It isn't accurate here!" And she stared over at him as if from some height, as if having mounted her anger under great sacrifice and duress she now poised at its very tip, and could greet with silence the expectant face he had turned to her, before plunging down the other side to explain.

But he blocked her descent. "Love is that pure for you? Love is that unmixed? It's all as clear as water to you, right?"

She watched the muddied, laden waves heave themselves upon the sand as if without energy to go further. "Chas, you ought to leave alone what you don't understand. Do as I do. When I'm with ..."

"Do as you do? Oh, thank you kindly." It was as though he'd catapulted toward her from snapped elastic. "Physician, heal thyself!"

She persevered. "When I'm with Troy, I ..."

"With Troy!" he laughed. And though he didn't finish his thought—for which, later, she felt grateful—he didn't need to. She and Troy had never dragged each other to hell and back with their teeth; they had never dug each other's grave with the force of their jaws alone. Nor had they launched themselves together, a nova designed to burn a purple flame and then explode into an ecstasy of starlit mystery. That wouldn't happen with Troy. She would never, in the midst of an argument, drive off and leave Troy standing, dressed only in surfer shorts, before a Pioneer Chicken in Mission Viejo—as she'd heard Annette had done to Chas. Or, at midnight, pull into the vast and empty parking lot at the Southcoast Plaza Mall so that she could argue with Troy and not be a traffic hazard, at last throwing her car keys across the shadowy blacktop, for him later to retrieve—like Darby had once made Chas do.

She wouldn't hurl a terra cotta bowl full of blueberries at the wall above Troy's head—Annette.

Or, over breakfast, fling her plate—frisbee-like—at him, all the pancakes spinning off in opposite directions—Darby.

And when a truce is called, not spend a day rolling about in the bedsheets like healthy young animals. That wouldn't happen with Troy.

With Troy there would be a mildness. He was a man who would never take the world between his legs and, well, *do* something with it: consume it, crack it open. He would be as familiar as worn furniture, as known as old shoes, as smooth under her hands as coins she'd constantly handled. But hers, *hers!*

She jerked from the thought as from an unexpected clap of thunder and even now—lying in a twilight of half-sleep, half-memory—it had the power to make her wince. As if torn from a dream back to life, she gaped about for several moments, not at first comprehending the tall spires and angels, the whiteness of the headstones and how they seemed to glitter in their unruly rows, the open grave and its canopy of orange, blue, and purple cracking in the wind. Seeing where she was—the picnic hamper lay at her elbow—and remembering where she'd been, made her face burn with the embarrassment she hadn't permitted herself to feel that day on the beach.

On that day, they had let it lie.

On that day, having been given the opportunity to see only what she wanted to see, she'd turned away.

When a stiff wind had blown up from the South, clouds of sand arose and swept off across the beach around them. At first, she had caught that motion only from the periphery of her vision: the drift, that veil of sand rising and then whipping about like gauze curtains. She thought she'd seen a ghost! But turning, her eyes cleared, and she saw something quite common: the wind creating sand spouts or what would on the Great Plains be called dust devils; the wind carrying bits of the beach away. Then she and Chas had both turned to retrace the half-mile or so back to the car, their shadows as if raking the sand behind them.

III

Next to her, the quilt was still wrinkled and bunched up in the form of his sleeping body, though Chas had already wandered down the hillside into the Garden of the Whispering Pines. She watched him occasionally pause before a tomb to read the inscription or, she thought, to admire some ornamental carving. After all, there was much to admire at Pinelawn.

Urns and obelisks overdraped with stone shrouds.

A soldier from the Crusades, 15 feet high, carved of black granite.

One lone pyramid, before which lay a sphinx-like statue.

An angel, sculpted of a porous white stone, whose wings arced in a kind of ecstasy from its body—but who, *beheaded* and *handless,* seemed to be rushing forth—enervated—into Glory.

He kept his back to her as he roamed about, his fists shoved in his jeans pockets; she imagined a smirk upon his face a smugness that made her skin burn hotter, but when he turned profile and Hazel caught a little of what was there, his features impressed her with their solemnity.

He knew!

Since that day on the beach—and how long before that?—he'd known about her and Troy. Known how short of. Known how convenient. Known as if he'd personally measured them in the act itself. Gauged them. Plumbed the depths. Sounded them for all that was there. Though she steadfastly wanted to believe that the Self is inaccessibly private, though she wanted to believe in mysteries the depth of which can never be calculated—the husband doesn't belong to the wife; not the wife to the husband; nor the lover to the other; children neither belong to the mother nor the father—though in this view the entire universe would rattle loose before her eyes, all its parts spinning off in their own directions, some spare ones clanking to the very bottom, and getting lost; in full sight of this—what she hoped unknowable, unfathomable, inaccessible—she nevertheless believed that *he* knew. It was all as clear as clean window glass, to his eyes, those blinking ones of the disinterested passerby drawn to plays of shadow, flickerings of light, movements just inside the proscenium arch of the curtains, the passerby who is unwittingly arrested by lives the only barrier of which is the pane itself. What she imagined she was doing *for* him, *despite* him, *through* him, *to* him and Darby and Annette—he'd already done. With *her*.

And since that day on the beach she had seen, if anything, how he kept her secret.

Without at first realizing that she'd leapt up from the quilt or even that she'd moved at all, she found herself standing bolt upright, staring off across the hills and headstones, but seeing as little as if the landscape had had all the opacity of marble. It was as though, without knowing it, she had been naked for some time; in all of God's earth there was no garment to don, no hole deep enough in which to hide! Not a religious woman, she nonetheless felt her heart pound with all the frenzied intensity of that experience, Southern Baptist-style. No, she couldn't say she believed in God and so on, but she would readily have said—even an hour ago—that she believed she knew about Love. Understood Love. It lay imminent in a way no god could for her, being suspended in the blood, tears, and semen of life—tasted on her tongue, silken under her fingers, redolent to her nostrils. She trusted it, swung from it as from a trapeze under which hangs no protective netting. And had never fallen, would never—in the aerial ballet she performed with Troy—drop like dead weight from any height. Face to face at the top, they'd meet as acrobats, their hands clasping with all the sureness of a grip well-studied, their fingers caressing, the wet parts of their bodies joining without mystery and peril. They would take no precautions, for there would be no danger. They, hurling themselves again and again through airy nothing, would have no secrets to keep, but would still, despite it all—even passionless to this extent—*burn.*

She watched Chas as he sauntered along; he had picked up a thin branch, stripped all the small twigs from it, and now holding it at one end, kicked the other end before him off the tip of his toe. In a moment the branch sprang as if animate from his hand; he leaned over, picked it up, and then began strolling along again with the stick before him, one end hopping up on the pavement as if he were walking some exuberant dog. There was nothing even covertly hostile in this act, yet something in her ganged up on the very boundaries of her body—like an army of fire that would erupt through her skin, rage across the cemetery, and engulf him.

He knew the size of it now—as did she.

Since that day on the beach she had seen him not only keep her secret, but how assiduously he went about the responsibility of keeping it as well. It was this, all unknown to her, which had spun, draped, hung, itself like a sticky yarn about them. It was unshared. It was unasked-for. But it was perhaps the thing which lifted her to ever greater heights in the rarified Strata of Love, the fine air there encouraging her to boast and brag of the view from that zenith as if she'd reached, all unassisted, the very top, top of the world. Not for the sake of exalting her—of shouldering her to that height and keeping her propped there as if under her own power—did he maintain their secret, it came down to her now, but rather for the sake of Darby and Annette, it being equally true that to sacrifice them would be to sacrifice himself. Most of all, though, it was—this secret assiduously kept—that she shouldn't begin to guess the bounds of what he saw.

Heat leapt through her body as brushfires overleap freeways.

He kept *her* secret. And the face he turned to her seemed often to say, "Because of that I know you'll keep mine."

It's what she wanted to read there in his features when he glanced over his shoulder at her approach. It's what she hoped to see engraved there as if in granite with hammer and chisel. She had woven a·path among the headstones and plots over toward the Garden of the Whispering Pines. But she hadn't so much *walked* toward him as she'd blazed a hot, smoking trail; were she to turn, she thought she'd see not footprints but singed grass where her feet had touched. Twice she'd faltered, stumbling first over the edge of a squat, over-draped stone urn and then an instant later, tripping over a decorative wreath, uprooting it so that she had to spend several moments rerooting its spindly, stilty legs. The self-congratulatory smirk which she had envisioned as set on his face—or petrified, or as hardened as if preserved in amber—had had plenty of time to manifest itself, just as a hideous specter, long-dead and flesh-ravaged, might from one of the graves across which she stumbled arise. When he glanced over his shoulder at her approach, she wanted to see vain pride in his eyes, yearned for it; she craved fiercely, as a natural desire of the body, the faintest glimmer of it there. She would have seen it had there not been a softness so richly represented, a defenselessness that she couldn't convert into anything to hate. For a long minute their eyes joined over the unsaid as if over roaring white water.

That was what they had: the words he didn't speak—as well as the ones she didn't. All gathered together and alphabetized, they constituted a strange lexicon, the pages of which neither dared finger, or an exotic language as yet untasted on any tongue. It—what both were aware of not saying—made for her the impression that she had given more intimately of herself to him than she could ever possibly to Troy, as Chas had given more to her than he might ever to Darby, or Annette, for that matter. It—what went unsaid—lay dammed up in some indeterminate space between them as a pool of impossibly still, bottomless blue which overlooks a tumbling falls. The threat that either she or he might blast this long silence—that either might speak—tossed about just below the surface of what they *did* say as the logs, driftwood, and other debris any teeming, watery turbulence threatens to beach.

"If I confessed to you that what goes on between Darby and me, or Annete and me, isn't love—well, what would it prove?"

"Prove?"

"Is it what you need?"

"Oh," she scoffed, "what I need!"

"Well—goddammit—you want *something* from me." Locked as his eyes were with hers over the unsaid, they nevertheless betrayed his desire to push beyond, to go all the way, to walk the plank over crashing, surging peril and then—arms flung wide—to leap in. "Don't you want anything at all?"

She felt herself tiptoeing along the shore. "Would you give me what I want, just like that, if you knew?"

It was a cannonball, when it came.

"What's with you, Hazel? What's happening? Why are you so afraid? If I swear that this isn't love Love—you know, Love with a capital 'L' Love—will you feel safe? It's like you're forcing the heathen to denounce their graven images so as to make your own god look good. What is this missionary zeal?"

"C'mon," she said.

"Spitting on the icons. Toppling all the statues. Breaking all the idols. Burning my temple and building yours over it!"

"Oh—Jesus!"

"Don't act so surprised." They stood faced off, he as rigid as the Crusader, she as still as the enervated angel. "Don't think I don't see what you're up to."

And it was hard, tension having settled about her shoulders and arms and in the tiny muscles of her face, not to feel that she had forced her limbs into a difficult posture which she godamn well meant to hold. Both she and Chas stood somewhat dwarfed by the slightly larger-than-life statues and obelisks about them, and it came up to her, as if from the earth itself, that in this garden of stone poses—given the rigidities they both so carefully guarded, given the intensity that seemed to have ossified about the joints, given their lives and their loves—they belonged.

She saw it, she saw everything. Sealed up, already petrified to some extent, they belonged. As his eyes bore into hers and hers into his—an act of mutual penetration that could only bind them more intimately each to the other—she imagined themselves as monuments erected over a single grave.

To what memory did they stand?

A one-word epitaph floated up as if out of a haze. Seeing it, reading it there in plain English, putting it—the word—together with the two poor stiffs represented, shed no light, moved her to no act, neither made it—"love"—more intelligible, or ironic or laughable, nor made her burn for another way of living so much as it merely made her burn: every hair on her head seemed a strand of fire.

But he was right there with her. "You can't pass judgement on my life with Annette and Darby. Why do you imagine that you know anything about it? Besides, you're not so clean. You're not so pure. You've got this little contradiction, too," he said, twisting the wedding ring on her finger.

Hazel tore her hand from his. On another occasion, one which seemed years ago and taking place on the planet Pluto, he'd said "Physician, heal thyself," and that statement had had the effect, she saw at once what she hadn't then, of wrenching her arm behind her back until it strained, tight and ready to pop from its socket. What he said, now, drove her to her knees.

And once uncapped, all that had churned just beneath the cool blue of the-things-he-said rose up like a great spuming tower of water. "Why do you stay with Troy, for that matter? Christ, you act like the two of you are *it*."

She glared at him.

"Like you've *made* love. Preserved it. Pickled it in a salt brine and put it on display. Don't you get tired, keeping up the pretense?"

"It's not a pretense."

"Why do *you* prolong it?"

"It's good. There's no reason not to prolong it. Chas, you don't understand..."

"Why you remain? No, I don't understand." Their voices tumbled down about each other as in a liturgical responsory.

"Well, at least I stay for good reasons."

"What are they?"

She said it through clenched teeth. "The right ones."

"What *are* the right reasons?"

The words were there. As if they'd waited just for the precise moment in which they would be needed, they were there. Dug up from some remote depth of the earth—and stiff from disuse—they nevertheless staggered forth. "Love"—she said it like it'd never been said before—"you understand? I love him, you see?"

But that phrase lacked most of its vitality; its impact did not outlive the last vibrations of her voice dying away in the air.

They stood blinking.

It was as if something deformed had been set in motion between them to totter off across Pinelawn, and of all the paths—straight and narrow—it might have chosen, it stumbled away in the general direction of that lone grave the workmen had opened. She watched as—all club-footed and gnarled—it fell in. It fell in—there were no cries or howls. It fell, and what went unuttered died in that hole, a perennial ghost: falling from this world into a never-never land of dragons, sea serpents, mayhem—falling again and again.

"Well, what is it? What's love?" He had planted himself before her, some obstacle to be gotten around.

She could wander about in that question forever, as if lost in some jungle—without a compass, without a machete, without any distinguishing features or landmarks to guide her. "What's love?" she repeated. "What is it?" No scenery along the way seemed in the least familiar, and her voice began to falter; it masked none of her doubt and misgivings but showed them exactly. "It's caring," she said. "It's mutual respect. And things shared." Here she cleared her throat, hoping to disguise her uneasiness.

"Things?" he prompted.

"Like *life* things," she told him.

It scattered away on the faintest of breezes.

All the same, this seemed to touch something responsive in Chas. He pretended not to notice her discomfort—or, perhaps, he really didn't notice it at all. Because he was nodding at her. "Tenderness," he continued. "Being enamored with. Having deep feelings for."

"Trusting," she said, eyeing him a little. Had he led her off their path, the one whose myriad footprints were exactly the size of her feet and his? Was this snarl of bittersweet, burdock, and tarweed *his* terrain? "Trusting and giving," she said.

"And how you think about the person all the time." *He* helped her. *He* understood.

"Affection, regard, and gentleness," Hazel said.

"Dignity."

"Thoughtfulness."

"Respect."

"Respect and happiness and—well—*love*," she told him.

"Well," he echoed, "love."

They sounded like people who, stranded for months in a deserted place and with little hope of any kind of rescue, had fed only on roots and grasses and seeds and were now naming their favorite foods.

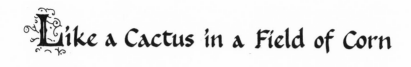

Like a Cactus in a Field of Corn

I am stretched out on the kitchen floor reading the newspaper the way I did as a girl, smudging my elbows with print, when Pops and Cora come in from watching the Yule pageant on TV. They fix some coffee, he pulling the ceramic canister down from a shelf, she lifting its lid; he fitting a paper filter into the coffeemaker, she spooning the coffee in. It's homey, it's warm. It's the kind of scene I'd be asked to shoot back at the Keller Agency, to sell X brand coffee to the burbs. "You've seen the ads?" she asks him.

He shakes his head, moves his foot near me. "I've been expecting something good from Kroger. It's time. They've been lousy since summer."

"Banquet frozen dinners," I say, turning a few pages. "Jeno's pizza. Egg rolls. God, these beef prices are grim."

"Well, Back East you've got the stockyards," Cora says. "All that good cornfed beef. You're lucky, you know." She nudges me with the toe of her slipper. "Here, the cows feast on chilis, citrus fruit, and Fuerte avocados. Makes for lousy standing rib roast." Her slippers are lavender terrycloth. She put them on when she got here, walking into my father's room in leather wedgies, walking out in them. "Oh, but who am I to tell you?" She turns, begins fiddling with the percolator.

Pops is reading the ad over my shoulder. "Mincemeat is good this week. Del Monte's number 402 cans are on sale for ninety-nine."

Cora pauses, contemplative. "Question: is that the 10 ounce or the 15½?"

"Well, that's a tremendous buy." Pops takes a few steps. He rubs his face then looks in the pantry, moves things. "Here's Van Camp's," he says, stretching the can at arm's length. "And Black Diamond." Cora draws her glasses up. "That's 15½ with a drained weight of 10¼ ounces. See? you have to look here."

"Don't I get one?" I ask.

He makes a mock kick in my direction and tells her that at home I do not shop Kroger, that I go to Jewel T, for convenience. "But you know, the Kroger label is good. There's quality there. Here's what happens, though. All the big chains are controlled by the Mafia. Hey, no fooling," he says, nodding. "I was talking to J. Vernon McGhee. It's how the A & P was run out of California. Remember all that jazz with Market Basket?"

I blink at him; Market Basket was the first to sell chicken wieners, and their produce was always cruddy—that's what I remember.

Cora squeals, does a slinky little dance across the tiles to him, and spreading his arms, slithers into them. "What did the A & P become after it left the west?"

He feigns the straightman. I sit up, fold the paper.

She smiles at both of us. "Just A."

Later, after she goes home, Pops shows me the award he was given by the City of Orange Society for the Practice of Law, an antique tulipwood gavel. He shows me the clocks he makes in the garage. At dinner, I give him a little something I've brought from Chicago: a tie of some variegated peach fabric. Family rumor has it that Pops has kept the same clothes in such good condition for so long that they've gone out of fashion and come back in again. Several times. He especially loves ties , has many, maybe 200 of them. A lot of his house is closed off and empty, the entire upstairs, for instance, where my room used to be; every closet there is choked with clothing. It's all *his* clothing, the doors sprung off their hinges what with the shirts, dinner jackets, the piles of rolled socks, the neckties draped on hangers. This morning when I arrived, he put my bag in his bedroom, deciding himself to sleep on the fold-out sofa. "No way," I said, dragging two of the suitcases back out, "because I don't want to inconvenience you."

A corner of the living room had been cleared to make way for the Christmas tree; it looked like an oasis of green amid all the blonde furnishings. "Nonsense, honey," he'd said. And he jutted his chin toward the corner. "Why, Joe'll keep me company."

I looked at Joe: a scotch pine, about seven-foot worth and still undecorated, near the patio doors; sunlight slanted through its branches like yellow smoke. I lit a cigarette and grinned.

Then Pops nodded to the bags at my feet. "Am I wrong, or is this more than just a little visit?"

But that's when we heard a scrabbling sound on the veranda, and Cora used her key to come in.

"It's a crazy tie," he says now, threading it through his collar and bringing the ends around.

"Well, I thought of you when I saw it."

He pats it down against his stomach. "We thank you." And then he's lifting lids, checking the oven, peeling prickly pears for dessert. I watch him stir the seviche, add more cilantro; he lifts the wooden spoon to my lips for a taste. All the cookbooks shelved just over the kitchen canisters are impeccably alphabetized; one lies open on the coffee table, a book mark stuck in it. "So that's what you did with your retirement. Became shockingly domestic," I say.

"How's that?" he says. "The way I see it, I was missing out on all the fun. And relaxation. I get a big kick out of cooking. Catching onto the styles. For instance, Julia Child is hung up on waxed paper. It's her nervous tic! She's always wrapping something in it. James Beard," he says "Saran. Hey, do you know the shallot joke?" Without my answering, he begins to recite it. "You may use shallots, chopped, in this vinaigrette. *Or* the white part of the green onion. *Or* if neither is readily available you may use onion, finely minced, parboiled for one minute, and drained through a wire strainer. Or you may omit them altogether." And then he collapses into laughter; tears glitter at the corners of his eyes. I smile along—but culinary humor, it doesn't really reach me.

While we eat, Pops quizzes me, just checking, the way you might check a newborn to make certain all its toes, its fingers are there. "Do you have a regular G.P.? What kind of health insurance do you carry? Have you found a dentist?"

I do a cheesey smile, move my lips so that even my bottom teeth show. Mother died when I was nine, so I've always relied on him to sympathize and listen to symptoms. He'll get around to asking when I'll move out of Wicker Park, a rough area. If I'm meeting some nice people. Did I ever get in touch with his old college buddy? He'll wonder aloud why I've never checked into that rooming house on Diversey, where mother once lived. All preparatory to learning why, festivities aside, I've come home.

The cutlery clicks. "And the job market. Did it get better?"

I settle back now, fit my shoulders to the chair. "Impossible. I shot stills for an ad agency. Then I"—the word's harsher than I intend—"quit." My eyes moisten.

Pops slaps a warm tortilla flat against his palm. Starting at the heel of his hand, he rolls it into a tight cone. Then he stuffs it with seviche and takes a big bite.

I try to imitate his actions, but my own tortilla, now cooled, splits. "Look, I'm a cactus in a cornfield there. I don't belong."

He speaks with his mouth full. "No cornfields in Chic, sugar. It's a world city. You're overlooking its qualities."

"They rotate crops—right?—when the soil is leeched of whatever nourishes them. I feel like I've depleted the region. I've exhausted it."

His voice is dreamy. "Your mother and I. We both had

tiny places near Lincoln Park. With Murphy beds. Met in the arboretum. In weather like this." He gazes out at the relentlessly golden California evening. The setting sun shines so brilliantly on the kitchen tiles that watery reflections dance across the ceiling.

"I missed the sun," I tell him.

It's as if he's awakened; he studies me a little. "You can miss the sun and not move 2500 miles away."

"I missed you."

A fine blush spreads across his features. "That's not reason enough, either Baby Doll."

The oven ticks, cooling.

We eat in silence.

"Well, what about that woman?" I ask. "What she wants with you. Does she think you've got money? What is she—30, or something? Should I bring her a rock album?"

His chair creaks as he leans back. "Cora's 47. She's a grandmother five times over. She's a widow."

"She got a glimpse of the house and decided you were loaded, or something?" I hold his gaze.

"And will she marry me? And will she steal your inheritance?" Resting both arms on either side of his plate, he scoots closer. "We'll never get married, because she'd lose her pension. Which, by the by, is more than I make each month. Now," he says, "Now, you see, we *could* live together . . ." He pauses as if just to scrutinize me, and I guess my expression is enough of what he expects. "Look, I always said the only reason to get married is if you're going to have kids."

My laugh is without mirth; it echoes in the pale, still light. "Whoah. When I was living with Lee you called it a 'shackup job'. Was that just a figure of speech?"

He puts his hands on his hips. "When you were living with Lee, I *said* I didn't want any illegitimate grandkids. And who cares what I say? I'm your father, yeah, but I've got my own life, for Christ's sake. Sugar, what's here for you? Will you face things? Or will you hide?"

I say hide.

He shoves back from the table. "You need to get out. Go see some people here. *Call* Lee, for all it matters."

"I am out. I am seeing people. I'm seeing you, right? And you're seeing me."

"Well, don't expect too much. Don't think I've done much. I haven't thought of activities for your diversion."

"Like I'm expecting anything? Here? I'll get on a fucking plane tomorr—" I'm digging half-moons in my palms with my nails.

"Well, well, isn't that pretty? *Now* we're cooking with gas. Yes'm."

The dinner mess lies between us. I stand as though rising from a bog, and begin to clear plates. Pops pulls out a pocket watch, clicks it open. "It wouldn't be a bad idea to swing by Kroger pretty soon. I don't have anything here, whatever sort of liquor you like."

Cora comes over about 9:00. I try to stay out of their way—do a load of wash, fix myself vodka martinis; I eat Fritos for the first time in five years—but the two don't seem entirely at ease. She's got a stack of Bingo cards from a couple nights back, the Specials: multi-colored squares that they play as bonus between regular Bingo. They're both on the sofa before the Franklin stove, the TV going, the tree a wedge of shadow in the corner. They're Monday morning quarterbacks, studying all the blotted numbers on these cards, talking about what might have been.

"I was sitting on number four for a long time," Pops says, rubbing his big thumb across a square.

When I pass by, Cora shows me Round the World: all the numbers on the periphery blotted; Corner to Corner: four dots only; the Big X: two slashing lines through the free center space. They are patient together. I wonder what happens when I leave the room. Maybe they swarm and grope each other, buttons popping, belts flying, shirttails yanked. Pops tries to help out. He says, "You two have something in common. Cora's first husband was a drill sergeant at Fort Ord. A G-17 when he passed on." He tells her how, convinced the G.I. Bill could prove handy later in life, I joined up after high school. He slaps my thigh with the stack of Bingo cards, his laughter the sound of something sawn off.

Well, it was handy.

I saw the fall of Saigon from a TV set on base in Stuttgart; I read about it in TIME like most vets my age, male and female, who knew that no matter how many had died there, *we* would live. Another E-3, a woman from Sun Valley, Idaho, accused me of fencing her stereo equipment, and flung from across the barracks a replica statuette of the Eiffel Tower which grazed me with its dagger tip before hanging like a dart in the wall. I biked through the alps. I ate octopus in Nice.

My lover never tired of hearing about California: San Francisco, Disneyland, orange groves—whatever TV and movies had exported about the place. He wanted to come home with me, and it almost could have been. After two years of that, after shredding NATO's classified paper, chauffeuring General Hiestand's dog to Baden Baden and Oberammergau, I returned alone, able to attend any university I desired. In Deutschland when you have drunk too much they say: *Sie haben zu tief in Ihrer Glas angeschauen.* It happened to me. I was free, and I learned the habit of peering too deeply into my glass, rushing about, as a student, to have several drinks each evening. What I saw in my glass after the oily vodka mixed made my brain arch, growing crystals and caves. At some point it all came crashing down. I quit school, quit drinking, started both again in Chic-town, at Pop's alma mater, and then left school for good. I held the sort of jobs you hold when there's nothing you want to do: sold photographic equipment in the Watertower. Trained to manage a One-Hour film developing store. Did all the things which conspired to lead me back like this to sit, a glass sweating in my hand. Pops doesn't drink, never did, except maybe during the war when they distilled whiskey from rubber. I bring the vodka in from the kitchen and stand it at my feet. He doesn't say anything, and because he doesn't *I* count how many drinks I've had. I frown in disapproval. "Basic at Fort Ord was quite an experience, " I say to Cora. She nods, cradles her jaw in the tripod of three fingers. We trade Army stories—old soldiers not fading away.

Later, when I go to bed, long after any child by all rights should have fallen asleep, I can hear them on the sofa. It's uninhibited, it's happy and loving, and it will, in a few minutes, end.

But that's cold comfort.

I wake late and ease up dreamily, realizing I've listened for several minutes, in sleep, to a steady thundering noise, like a stampede, rumble in from the living room. I leap off the mattress. The Richter scale jumps before my eyes; I see needles scribbling the earth's haywire EKG on graph paper. When I rush down the hall, I find Cora and Pops dancing though there is no music. Tea cups jangle in the hutch; the bristly limbs of the scotch pine tremble. Cora kicks her legs high. He swings her around, stops her, starts again.

"What—?" I say, my heart stilled. The sofa is folded back into itself, homely needlepoint cushions stationed at either end.

Pops twirls her into a corner and then comes for me. He slips his arms around my waist and we take off near the table. He's warm. His hands press firmly on my back. There seems to be a pattern to what he's doing, but I don't follow it. I jump up and down, bump his knees, stumble on his feet. "Hold 'er neut' there, Andy," he says. He tries to show me a step, gazing not at my feet, but deeply into my eyes, speaking softly. But I spin out of his arms, skip into the kitchen.

"Call someone for tonight," he says. "We're all going dancing!" They promenade wildly near the refrigerator. Cora throws herself into frantic solo steps, and I look away.

"You forgot about my wooden leg," I mutter. I pour some coffee, stare out the window at the lone palm; its fronds are so dry they make a crazed, thrashing sound in the breeze.

Standing just beneath is the ceramic Santa statue.

Yesterday, after reading the newspaper and sliding it back on top the refrigerator, I caught sight of the statuette for the first time; I burst out laughing, thinking it some joke — Santa squats under date palm — but Pops gave his head a small, fast shake and pressed his finger to his lips. It all dawned slowly. Cora stood not three feet away fiddling with the coffeemaker; it was just a hop, skip, and a jump to see her in her non-credit ceramics class, in a smock, brushing the glaze on.

Now, Pops massages my shoulders with his hot, sweating hands; he's catching his breath. "Wooden leg? Or *hollow?* 'Cause you put a dent in that bottle, Baby Doll."

My cheeks burn. I whirl from his hands as if ripping something from them. Cora's still breathing heavily. "Let it go, Counselor. C'mon. Let's talk about Christmas."

He scoops her into his arms and rubs his chin along her neck; I know that sandpaper feel. But his eyes haven't left mine as he says, "Relax. Don't get all nervous and jerky. Because you know what?"

She and I both say "What?" though she's staring down at her slippers.

"We like you," he says.

It's as if he's given her a rare treasure. "You goodie-good," she says, stroking his cheek.

They rumble off into other rooms — I hear them hit furniture. I hear something break, but they don't stop.

When they've gone out for groceries, I sit at the table, look up old loves in the phone book. It's maddening how they're all still here. So accessible, out front for anyone to find. Page after page—all the names I ever had uses for, all the names to form in the throat! And the faces, stuck a long time in memory, remembered at those smothering, expectant moments when we fell one over the other into back seats across Orange County, discovering things. I listen to the crackle of pages. It's as if I've come home to look at these names. The listing for Paul Biagi has an office number and extension printed just below and then, indented, a listing for "children's phone." For God's sake, my breathing's hard. What has happened, I wonder. What sort of life can this be? Oh, Paul, I want to say. I want to call him, to call his children, and find out.

I come across Lee's number and see he's still living in the tabby house he bought with family money, an ugly one-story affair which looks like common stucco but really is crushed shell and mortar. I ruined a black sweater, brushing up against the outer wall, all that chalky white coming off like powder. Lying awake there, thinking about the walls, the supports under the kitchen floor, I could see it all crumbling into a mountain of dust around me. Lee worried me. Those last few weeks we lay cold together. Tight. Small, small. At that time I worked in the photo lab at the V. A., making slides for presentations and research. He had quit work. During the day he sat in the dining alcove composing music no one would ever play, striking keys on the piano and that one key, so necessary to his arrangements, which was broken or out of alignment, which simply pounded its felt hammer against more felt or something deadening, missing the strings, and made a thumping sound, a cut-off sound, sudden like realization, like amputation, a sound I could not bear. In his music there was the thump and then silence, like snow, like softness, silence held for a beat, a quarter-beat—whatever its function—as we both, I half a house away, supplied the missing sound. That note—either flat, sharp, or natural—I could never find it. When alone, I ran my fingers over the keyboard, winding them in stairstep fashion, a spidery motion, and heard only the music trailing up the scale, unbroken. Normal.

I dial and wait, afraid he won't be there—as though he *should* be! But when he answers I realize I haven't thought of anything witty to say. "It's me," I begin. "I'm back. I'd like to see you. Maybe for dinner?"

There's a long hesitation. Then he says, "Betsy? Janet? Ellen? Carol? Anna? Martha? Sal?" And he laughs. I laugh, too, remembering.

Pops comes home late in the afternoon. I'm taking a bath, moving the water with my knees, staring up at the frosted skylight. My skin is hot and pink; sunshine streams down like a liquid. He's humming something. He's alone.

When he knocks on the door, he says, "What do you have going for tonight?"

I tell him I'll be busy, that he should count me out of his plans.

He starts to walk away, then comes back. "Listen, I checked around. You might be able to get some camera-work fulltime at Crescent Advertising. J. Vernon McGhee's put me on to something."

"Oh, crap," I say. I sink low with my legs scrunched so my earlobes touch water.

"What?" He bumps close to the door.

I lift my hands and tilt them, let the drops roll down like pearls. A creamy soap film floats around me. "I said—I don't know—oh, crap, or something."

"Because I don't know how long you plan to stay." His voice rises. "This might not be a bad idea."

I arch forward, sloshing water back and forth against the tile and fixtures. A wave flops over the side and makes a pool in the corner. "Who the hell is this McGhee character?" I ask when the swirling settles. "Some hot dog?" But Pops has already moved down the hall. I hear the pantry door.

After a while I stand, my skin shiny. I listen at the door, a puddle forming around my feet. I peer out, wait. It is so still. A sudden flicker of blues and greens lights up the living room doorway, then blinks out to be replaced ten seconds later with a twilight of yellows and reds. and then both at once: a rainbow glow issuing forth. The bulbs click together as he tests the strands of Christmas lights.

I run fresh water and slide back into the tub.

When we lived together in the tabby house, Lee worked at a computer keyboard by day, the green terminal shining down on his skin. I toiled away at the V. A., making slides of dissections: kidneys, arteries, muscle fiber, fatty tissue, tendons. Once, I was commissioned to do a histology, the cross-section of a heart, all its chambers enhanced with purple photographic dye; a Hasselblad was mounted on a lift above the gurney. I cranked it down low, brought the organ into focus. "Say cheese," I said. Slide smears, particles, ovum, follicles, marrow, joint, gray matter—I photographed body *portions* only; not out of all those pieces could I make man. So I took to studying Lee, doing nudes, full-figures, fashion plates; I stood in the darkroom waiting for his image gradually to rise up out of the chemicals.

Did I take enough photos to steal his soul? Or was it left behind in the silver salts which floated to the bottom of the developing tray? We used to joke about it.

But it was no joke, what he lost. At home he sat slumped over his other keyboard, the metronome clicking away, head resting against the steeple of his hands. So it was restorative, my work in the dark: I resurrected him. And after reproducing the hacked-at organs, the gobbets of flesh all day—body parts recognizable only under a surgeon's gaze—resurrection mattered. Did I, in the rush to make something whole, see only what I wanted to see? Chest as wide as a file cabinet. Waspwaist. Calves the size of my thighs, forearms the size of my calves. The tip of his penis a velvety flower bud. Was I isolatory? One day, toward the end, he snatched up a handful of my photos and flung them; they fell like birds. "That's the problem," he cried; he plucked a picture from between the cushions of the sofa. "Only my pubic hair is in focus."

What I did I did for myself.

Lee's tabby house didn't collapse into a mountain of dust, but *we* did. I surfaced in Chic-town. Phone calls at odd hours of the night always made me think I'd be getting word of his suicide...

He comes over.

Not having decided before now how to greet him, I find myself hugging him close and kissing the smooth skin just beneath his ear. The shirt he's wearing is so stiff and new its collar scrapes my cheek.

"You remembered how to get here!" I say. "Didn't get lost on any streets? Didn't have to stop for directions?"

"Who forgets? *You've* been away. Did *you?*"

This ambiguous reply annoys me. "I mean it's been quite a while," I say. "Hasn't it?"

"Five years? Five years out of your long life?" And he laughs.

That's not an answer, I think, my heart thumping.

He saunters past me into the room. "Pops is out," I say.

"Dancing."

"Doesn't stop, does he?" Lee says, and I turn further to glance at him. His smile—white, wide—gives nothing.

"Pretty," he says, nodding to the tree in the corner. Silver garlands bristle from its already bushy limbs; the lighted bulbs cast an aurora of reds, blues, and greens.

He looks at it, I look at him. An elaborately-tooled squash blossom necklace rests against his chest, and he wears wide cabochon cuffs at his wrists; there's a tiny turquoise in his earlobe, and a braided bola tie round his neck. Its slide is a silver nugget and hangs at his solar plexus. I touch the bola's tips, the metal beads just slightly cold. It's hard to believe that while a storm raged over Lake Michigan I dumped all those photos off the Belmont Harbor breakwater, down into turbulent waters. "This is nice," I tell him.

"Useful," he says, yanking it up, noose-like, around his throat.

There is a difference between ordinary, relaxed laughter and the broken, tight sort that rises convulsively in my throat.

In the kitchen, I check the roast while he mixes a couple drinks. His hands are soft-looking. *He* remembers where things are: the Old Fashioned glasses, the stirrers; last night I spent five minutes looking. "So you came back. And it's like you were never here in the first place." He chuckles. "Maybe you've got the wrong house." We sip our drinks and he tells me about his life, about a woman he wants to marry who lives out in Indio, who teaches at College of the Desert. He's moving there, he says. In January. "To live forever," he says. He shakes his head. "You know how I always wanted to live on the desert. I need hard country. Rock. I need little cloud cover, direct sunlight overhead. Location works on your spirit—I truly believe this." A dart of white fire flashes from the wide silver cuff as he gestures. I don't remember these things; I remember the truncated music, the stultifying sadness. "For right now, that kind of rough, desert terrain, hard mountains, and so on, will help to restore my soul." He smiles at the image in his mind. "And she's got these two incredible kids."

But his music?

An expression of pure tranquility crosses Lee's features as he talks about how he wanted to get rich, how he wanted people to like him: lots of money, lots of people. "Clothes. Cars. Houses. Vacations." He stretches back, hands linked behind his head. "But those weren't the only things I wanted. In fact, they were dramatically unimportant, believe it or not. The less I thought of them, the less music meant to me. I gave it up."

But there *was* self-expression.

"Now I make jewelry. I express myself that way. You see? Out there," and he gestures to some place just beyond the page of black that is the kitchen window, "I'll be closer to my materials. The desert floor is 15% mineral, 7% ore, and 78% quartz. It's just waiting for me to make something beautiful of it."

"So, that explains it," I say, tracing a necklace and necktie around my throat with my finger.

He nods. "That explains it."

We sit down to our salads, eating and reminiscing. I leap up occasionally to check things and then to bring it all over to the table. We gossip about people we've known: their pregnancies, drug addictions, bankruptcies, deaths. Afterward, we remain at the table with our dirty plates. Outside it's absolutely still, and the night black: the light thrown from just inside the living room archway is like what is left when the darkness is scraped away: layers of blue, red, and green. I sit back, spinning into the vodka; I tell him I'm just visiting, that I don't know how long I'd be welcome here besides.

He asks what Pops says.

I shrug. "I guess I was expecting to be waited on a little more. Or that life would revolve more around me. That I'd get more attention. That he'd forget he had a life and be daddy again. He's certainly got a life," I say, my eyes falling on a crocheted pot holder which I know to be Cora's handiwork.

My voice sounds thickly ironic, and Lee frowns, bewildered. "What? Is he smuggling steroids across the border? Burying bodies in shallow graves?"

His cigarette rests in the ashtray, its smoke such a straight and silvery thread leading up to the ceiling it's as if it hangs suspended from a string. "I just want to mope and feel sorry for myself," I say.

"Well, that isn't exactly criminal," he begins.

"Oh, God," I say with a certain heat, for looking at him I see only the jewelry; he's such an agglomeration of silver and stone . . . ! I rise, put our plates in the sink. "I'm sure that it *is* criminal," I say, "Somewhere." A thumbnail moon dangles high up; it cuts a path of white in the night.

He stands, places his hands on my shoulders. "I know you," he whispers.

His reflection appears there in the black pane before me, as if floating just below the surface, or as if etched in gray tones to its underside, and it's so much of what I used to see rise up from chemicals in the dark that I look away. "No, you don't know me. It was different then."

"Your daddy's happy," he says. "He's got a lady. Why, there's *Lady* all over this room." And he gazes about, catching the high points: curtains, wallpaper, the decorative ceramic plates. "It's something *you're* probably going to have to . . . "

"Oh, stop! It's easy for you to know who you are. Look! You've got the costume to wear." My fingers tangle with the ends of the tie round his neck. "It's your get-up!"

We stand faced off, and the room slows, seems to stop, like something, once spun out to its snapping point, which can only wind back in. Then Lee jerks the silver nugget down and yanks the bola up over his head; it clangs against the counter when he flings it, and a chip of tile flies up.

Our embrace is like a grapple.

The headboard bangs against the wall; the bed undresses itself, all its silver ticking lying naked in the moonlight. Beyond the window, the palm makes a crazed, thrashing sound. Soon it is as if I am out there, buffeted on the wind, and riding it like a surf that will in a moment explode and send me tumbling end over end. The thrashing recedes gradually.

After, we doze. I weave in and out of sleep, waking at some point near midnight to find Lee's face hovering near. "She's lively," he mutters.

I look at his face until it dissolves into darkness and I fall back a long time—but sounds come from the living room. I groan. "Don't listen to that."

He prods me with his thumb. "So there's a stepmother on the horizon, eh? Or maybe in the woodpile?"

"*Co*ra. She makes his tater wet."

His laughter is suppressed like a sneeze. "Aren't you a real sweetheart."

I stretch, feel the soft moisture of his penis against my thigh. He, listening, begins to giggle. "Goddammit," I say.

"I'm sorry." And he stuffs the sheet over his mouth.

Then even I smile. "She screams."

"Oh, no."

"Yes."

"I can't wait."

"Well, it's not a scream. It's restrained. But if I weren't here..."

Lee punches me in play. "So leave, right? And quit spoiling his sex life."

I raise up on my forearms. "No, I wouldn't think that that's..."

"Shhh, shhhh," he says, his hand near my mouth. The house grows deeply silent; a few moments pass. Then there are the voices: low, quick. "Well, how the hell was I to know?" I think is what Cora says. There is muttering that gets louder for several minutes; I shrink down in the sheets. But Lee narrates it all for me, as if translating an opera. "She loves him, yes, but it's, it's... Not like before? he asks. This mattress. Her Back. *Hers? His,* he says." After a bit there is the front door, then a cabinet bangs in the kitchen. Lee rubs his hand down my spine. "No offense, my dear, but I believe you're the third wheel here."

By that time I pretend I'm already dozing, and then, as the house settles, I really do fall asleep. At what hour near dawn do we, as if rising up in a mutual dream, go to the kitchen door? The moon, just setting, drapes the Saddleback hills in silver. Lee passes from the patio to the yard and, because I'm watching, overleaps the Santa statuette next to the palm before disappearing into darkness. In my dream he doesn't stop, not for the San Bernadino mountain range, not for the miles of strangled freeways, or the Los Angeles Aqueduct, until he reaches the sun and can see his footprints as scars he's left behind.

Which seems still to leave me with the wounds.

This is the thought that yanks me out of sleep.

The trail of pain I've dug with my heels from the heartland to the west gapes before me, a magnificent canal: blood blackened on its ragged edges. Everything I've ever lost parades before my eyes: pocket change in washing machines, views from the windows of all the apartments I've rented, dignity, face, the ground I've lost, the memories, the heart. I think of the people—neighbors, landlords, grocers, hair stylists, doctors—I've left behind. And—friends, lovers—those who meant more than my hasty parting made it seem. It's a waking nightmare: living parts of me still languish in Chicago, in Stuttgart, in Orange County; they obligate me like children I've abandoned, like newborns in dumpsters, or those left lying in the waste cans of women's rooms. They have every right to implore; they have every right to look at me through eyes that condemn. I have lived like a coward, though I am not a coward.

"My bastards, my poor bastards," I whisper. My eyes fill and then spill over. It's a sickly cry. Tears leak slowly down both cheeks; even gravity won't hurry them.

And once started there seems no end. I'm like a stone virgin suddenly come to life to weep. Tears drizzle down my face as I brush my teeth. The skylight is a brilliant square of white which pours dazzling sun down on the fixtures and casts my big shadow across the floor; one tear splashes, like a raindrop, on the darkened tiles. It's not until I kneel in the tub, forehead touching the cool porcelain, the blast of water from the faucet like surf pounding my head and neck, that it ends, and I remain crouched low like that, spent.

The first thing I notice is the minty smell of Ben Gay, and then the pinched tube of it lying next to the coffeemaker. For his back.

The second thing I notice is the tiny jar of porcelain paste standing on the kitchen counter and where it's been newly applied to one of the tiles. I remember the arc Lee's arm made, that flash of silver. Sight of this chip, so efficiently repaired, nettles me. I blow on my coffee, fling the teaspoon into the sink, and then wander on out to the living room where Pops has been humming for several minutes. I tell him I want to pay for the broken tile.

An open box of icicles lies on the hassock; he approches the Christmas tree, only a few twisting strands draped over his hand. After he's hung those he stands back, studies all the silver floss, and then walks toward the hassock for some more. As he stoops down, he glances up at me. "Relax, Baby Doll." And he asks if I'd like huevos rancheros for breakfast.

My temples throb. I insist that he allow me to pay for the tile, tell him I'll not take no for an answer, even stalk around the furniture, looking for my purse. I grab one of the needle-point cushions and dash it, with real force, against the sofa.

"Well, those tiles were handmade. Ceramic," he says. "Made expressly for me." The icicles shimmer as he hangs them. "So nevermind. Listen. I checked that advertising thing. It's part-time. I don't know what you want. If that's your interest."

I say I'm not sure if I'll be around long enough for it to make a difference anyway.

He stands before the tree, contemplative. "That McGhee —he's steered me wrong before."

Having found my purse I now slam it to the carpet. All

the tampons, sugar-free gum, lone cigarettes, and lipsticks roll out. "J. Vernon McGhee," I mutter, "that's all I ever hear." On my knees I begin tossing the mess back in, and when I rise Pops has turned around, pulled something from his pocket which he now dangles before my eyes.

A chunk of brilliance sways in the air.

"You trying to turn me into a cowboy?" he says. But before I can snatch the bola from him he hangs it round his neck and yanks the silver nugget up. "Uh uh," he says, "it's mine now. Yes, indeed. Cora and I are going out to Palm Springs for New Year's Eve. Ooooooh, I'll fit right in. Soy vaquero hermosa con una mujera encantada. Se puedo bailar, mi hermosita?"

"You can choke on it," I say.

As I turn to leave the room, he clamps his hand around my arm and jerks me back to him. A lock of hair falls down over his left eye. Just behind, the tree ornaments clink together, in sympathy. "Free me," he says.

I shake my head, try to twist from his grip. *"Free me,"* he says, clasping me now with both hands, my breasts pressed to his chest. "I'm 67 years old, and I'm your father. I love you, Baby. But I don't know what to do about it. What do I do? Adopt you? Make love to you?"

The sound that rises from me is like a wail. And then I do wrench away.

Subtle air currents stir about the room, the icicles flashing tiny darts of fire as they twine from the tree. Sunlight drifts through the branches like gold vapor.

Pops remains implacably there, his hands stuck out before him as if he still held me, his whisper an entreaty I'll not forget. "Just who do you think I am?"

On Mu

The flowers he'd brought her had no sex organs. They were shaped like irises, or what she'd always heard people call flags, but the ones she remembered shooting up through her girlhood were bearded at their centerpoints and resplendent with stiff, pollen-dusted stalks there. Ivy stared deep into the cone of one's pedicel and saw only a hole, purple tapering off to dusky indigo and then darkness. In the next, a waterdrop nestled at the center, clasped, like a jewel is in the prongs of a ring, by the petal walls. But—no stamen, no bulge of ovary. What prick in a hot house took all pleasure from these flowers? she wondered.

They were very pretty, all the same.

He leaned forward and buried his face among them, breathing audibly, then glanced up at her, his eyes an unusual hue—a living color; she thought of sea green phosphor.

"Can you go on break now?" he asked.

Ivy glanced at her watch. "Yeah," she said. She looked around. "I know where we can talk."

They were standing on an open-air mezzanine at Orange Coast Mortuary; she lead him back inside. The building resembled a Georgian mansion: heavy white pillars supporting the ceiling, galleries leading from the foyer that was of richly-veined marble and lighted with a multi-tiered chandelier of slender, six-sided crystals. It was where she served her embalming apprenticeship, neutralizing the effects of death, going beyond the book-learning she'd acquired while studying mortuary science, finding herself out, too. He had come to Orange Coast a couple times before, to pick her up after work, or for lunch, but hadn't gone beyond the entryway. Now, she heard his hushed footsteps as he followed her down a long corridor, the carpet springy underfoot. Most of the slumber rooms at Orange Coast had viewings scheduled, their wide double doors blank and discreet as they passed, but this smaller one in the back was free until tomorrow. She was still working on its body—a cancer death. It was laid out in the neat, expansive laboratory just below, one vertical incision in its side and a horizontal one—razor-sawn—across its crown.

Ivy clicked open the door and they walked in. Even devoid of flowers the room still suggested them: bare table tops, spaces between chairs, and especially the alcove where the casket would lie on its skirted gurney.

He stood in the center of the room with her. "Wow," he said. "Fragrant."

The scent permeated everything—as if flower ghosts still lingered, awaiting more of their kind.

So these irises would fit right in.

Ivy looked at the bouquet. "Well, thank you," she said.

She plucked the card from within the ferns, and he watched as she opened it.

"I'm sorry I made those accusations about Mu," the message read in a cool, steady script. "Please forgive me." And instead of signing his name, he'd drawn a bouquet of tall stalks topped with flame and gold disc-shaped petals.

The cosmos.

He'd always said his mother called him Cosmos for the flower, not for the orderly, harmonious universe in which she hoped he might live. Ivy thought with its flat, satellite-like petals it was probably named for the universe, anyway.

She stuck the card back among the ferns and stared into his eyes, the green. When at her apartment, or seated across the table from her in a restaurant, he always *looked* at her hands—as if expecting to see her work of the day there. He said he worried about the chemicals: her breathing them, the possibility of their burning her skin. She knew he meant he worried about how the hell she could stand there all day touching something—flesh, human—gone stone cold. Ivy made no attempt to hide her hands, which were always fresh-scrubbed and pink from the scrupulous cleanliness of the work; she hoped he would understand. But when the words all slipped away, she was left only with the feeling. "At first there's the temptation to feel for a pulse—but that passes."

He looked at her. "And it's replaced by what?"

"By—well, *it*. The beauty of it. It's a perpetuation, what I do. I entomb them *in the flesh*. Then they're entombed in the ground," was the best she could do at those moments.

None of it comforted him. "What you do is more for the living than the dead."

"Well, some of it. So far as we know. There's a lot we don't."

"Don't?"

"Don't know about them. I mean the dead."

He just stood before her, looking uneasy, as if she'd spoken not English but a gibberish so encrypted he could never hope to transform. Now, Ivy noticed he didn't turn his back to the gabled end of the room where tomorrow she'd wheel in her handiwork: its eyelids forever sealed, layers of clothing bought for just this purpose covering the indelible dye marks used in radiation treatment, make-up not hiding too well the ashen aftereffect of chemotherapy. This was a tough one.

"I was beginning to see Lemurians under the bed," Cosmos said.

She shrugged. *"In* the bed."

He raked his fingers back through his hair, rubbed his hands against his mint-colored Oxford cloth shirt, retucked it into his tennis shorts. As he moved she could see the hand-tooled squash blossom necklace just inside his open collar. It lay almost flush with his skin, as if cleaving to him, or as if lying in the pattern it had grown, round his neck, before it turned to silver. He was a certified gemologist—with the patience to toil over trifles: ½ carat weight, a Troy ounce here and there—and had worked 10 semi-precious stones into the necklace. Unfaceted ones, or *rough*—because "I'd view the world through a smooth jewel, if I could," he'd told her—without the corners and angles that were difficult to see beyond.

And now the emerald, sapphire, and peridot sparkled out at her. Ivy glanced away, because he'd always told her jewels could prophesy, could showcase destiny, and she wasn't certain if at this moment she wanted to know what lay immediately ahead. It was bad enough that the ruby she wore round her neck kept trying to leap from her body. This had happened twice, in bed—once alone and once not, but each time she'd rolled over in the sheets and found the gem, emancipated, and then her serpentine strand lying innocently by.

Before Cosmos had made the necklace, she requested a moonstone but he mounted her birthstone in the setting instead, because wearing the stone of some other month, he said, brought bad luck. When he showed up he gave her a marquise-cut *yellow* gem, though, not a ruby.

"You trying to sour my luck?" she said. "This is a *topaz*," she told him.

"No," he said. "That's not so." He let her examine it under his jewelers glass. "It's a ruby," he said. "A yellow ruby. Identical VSU to other rubies. The only thing harder than a ruby is carborundum. And the diamond. I mean, I've even cut diamonds with rubies. The topaz is a soft stone, comparatively."

Ivy thought gazing through that small eyepiece at an 8mm jewel would be a reduction—so she squinted into the crystal with that expectation. And saw a place where it seemed the secrets of life were housed in clean, mathematical stillness, down long hallways. Her eye roamed the yellow, glossy floor, and the passages that angled off from some center or core, that seemed to draw energy away from the core.

An entire silent galaxy existed within boundaries no longer apparent to her, and she imagined walking down the concourse of the ruby—dancing its long length—the sound of her footsteps nestled in a dense, soft-seeming quiet.

"They aren't just red," he told her, his voice lulling and coming as if from a soothing distance. "There are orange ones. Blue. I've seen pink. I'm not joking," he said when she opened both eyes to look at him. "Someone just decided the red ones were precious."

She thumped the jeweler's glass against her palm. "It is rare?" she said.

He thought for a moment. "Overlooked," he told her. "Unappreciated," he said. "They *are* out there. But I swear you won't find another yellow one within a 100 mile radius. Not in L.A. County, or San Diego County. Not in Riverside County, either," he said.

Ivy held it up to her throat on its golden link.

Using one knuckle, he rubbed the area just above her breast bone where the stone would rest once she hung it round her neck.

He could do that; he had those nice touches. They transported her. He had fashioned an elaborately irresistible world—an alternative to this one—and then, like a gentleman, had held back its flap, so she could enter first. But it had tightened and choked in around her like the neck of the drawstring bag in which he kept his rare minerals and gems. It was beyond sad, how that world had its kick.

Now, Ivy glanced up at Cosmos. He believed souls inhabited jewels—so she would never tell him about how her ruby kept trying to make its escape, kept trying to slide in the sheets away, because he might interpret its actions as suicide.

And what if it only wanted to leap free of her body?

"I was wrong," he said, his voice low. "All that stuff about Mu—that crap," he said, "is wrong. I misinterpreted it," he told her. "I *know* you weren't going out on me."

"Look, I've had time to dwell on this, too," she said. "You revealed more about yourself—and the way you think—when you manufactured that bullshit than anything."

He stood absolutely still, as she had seen stunned, hunted animals who hope to blend into the landscape do. And the way his gemstones glittered out at her could mean anything at all.

"I bungled some information, believe it or not. Listen to me, Ivy. I mislead myself." He nodded to the bouquet in her hand. "I want to make peace."

She glanced down to the array of purple, gold, white—and especially the green. But—sexless flowers. That was no kind of gift. And in a mortuary!

When she moved to set them on a side table, though, she saw they weren't *cut* flowers at all—but bulbs, in a planter; instructions told how to transplant them outside later in the fall.

Anger surged in her as she looked from the irises to Cosmos's face.

"Goddammit all," she said.

He always gave living gifts.

The cactus for her front yard.

A sourdough starter which, dating back to 1939, was old enough to be her mother.

A blue budgie parakeet called James.

The gifts he gave had a way of obligating her, of pilfering some portion of her time and care. They made demands of her. Pressed, solicited. Asked things. Wanted.

And they died.

Because saguaros couldn't thrive in Orange County, the cactus in her front yard had shriveled, died upright. That lump of sourdough had rotted and dried out in her refrigerator, from disuse. Later, James *keeled* over in his cage, dead of a feather disease.

Cosmos's gifts thieved, took themselves back.

Anymore she couldn't really look at a live thing given by him without seeing its eventual death-ravaged end. And there wasn't a goddamn thing peaceful about death: eyes rolled up under the lids, mouth wide open, jaw as if forcibly yanked down, arms pulled back, chest thrust out pigeon-style, skin the color of gun metal, fingers and toes like stiff, splayed talons. As an embalmer at Orange Coast, Ivy's art lay in substituting the effects of rigor with the more natural ones formaldehyde brought on.

She remedied death.

In that long room of ceramic tile and stainless, soon after she'd applied the needle, the eyes rolled back; it became possible to close the mouth. Joints loosened. Gradually the knuckles became pink, as if a private sun were rising just beneath the skin. And the body grew pliable again.

It was as if she were giving birth, in giving life back to the dead. What she did, when embalming, was a correction—but she couldn't remedy the lives Cosmos brought. They chose to die, and then after would not be resurrected.

Now, Ivy bumped against the table the planter sat on, and

the irises shivered. Christ God Almighty—would you water them, or hurl them against the wall?

Cosmos moved cautiously before her, his hands out, palms up—as if he wanted her to take something from them. "I've got to amend what I said. About the destruction of Mu. And whatever part you had in it. Even about things Cayce prophesied. Like whether California will slide into the ocean." He shook his head, laughing at himself. "It was all incorrect. *I* see that now. I botched every last bit of it," he said. He waved his hands in the general direction of the bouquet. "Please accept this in the spirit in which it's given," he said.

"Which spirit is that?" she wondered. *Or whose?* Because for him that word didn't mean just one thing. After all, he had the tradition, the history. He'd grown up, dragged to Camp Chesterfield every other week—where they had the materializations, the manifestations. He'd sat there, clutching the back of a pew so tightly his hands were big white fists, and waiting for the face of someone, long dead, to appear, hologram-like, before him. His mother had received a Life-Reading from Edgar Cayce, the sleeping prophet, in which she was advised to savor the juice of 30 potatoes—skins only—in order to retain her natural hair color. He also suggested she let water mix with her salivary glands before swallowing it. *"Chew* it. Four times," he told her. "Masticate it," is what he said. When Cosmos's father had a heart attack, and died, the family expressed genuine grief. But—as ye shall sow, so shall ye reap—it was also understood that "Self meets self," that the soul, or entity, which was his father, had to make good on its karmic debt, had to sacrifice for the errors it had accrued in past lives. Cosmos had corresponded with Hugh Lynn Cayce and still followed the Cayce diet, refusing to eat grapefruit and grains at the same meal. He adhered very strictly to Cayce's dictums.

"Never fall asleep with the moon shining on your face," a Medium had once told him—and Ivy was familiar with the ritual he performed before bedtime, how he adjusted the venetian blinds just so, some light still falling about the floor, making diamond patterns on the carpet, but not shining anywhere near his face. The first time he slept over at her apartment he asked her to arrange the curtains a little bit.

"Bunch them up," he said.

At that point they were still becoming accustomed to each other's intimate habits, and though she didn't know him well, there were things Ivy loved: he somersaulted out of bed in the morning like a circus performer. And he always brought back to her a plate of raisin toast, all stacked up, maybe 6 slices—and buttered on *both* sides.

"Ahh," she'd said once, "Now I know."

He slid across the mattress to her. "Know what?"

She held a slice of toast before him so he could admire how riddled with raisins it was, how perfectly marbled throughout with thick cinnamon sugar whorls. She said, "Which side it's buttered on."

That first time, though, at her place, he'd directed her to rearrange the curtains. When she frowned, he explained his predilection.

Ivy leapt up out of bed, held the flimsy mesh material aside to show him. "It's a streetlight," she said. A shaft of white sliced across the mattress, an aura of yellow fringing its edges.

He blinked out at it for several moments, as if seeking to remember all the Medium had ever said about artificial, incandescent light, and then sighed, falling back into the sheets, relieved.

"What'll happen if you fall asleep with the moon on your face?" she'd asked the next morning. They were sitting up in bed, a plate of 3 minute eggs between them, and sharing a mug of pitchy black coffee. She'd already watched him peel a banana horizontally. He split the skin at its centerpoint with his thumbnail and then *undressed* it, as if it were a doll. As if removing its overcoat, not its pants.

He shot her a look.

"Bad for the soul," he said, "Very bad."

Cosmos' dedication to his faith, and to Cayce's doctrine, had always impressed her, his constancy and devotion still impressed her—but he wasn't free.

He gargled his water before swallowing.

He ate three almonds every day.

God knows how he'd peel an orange.

What's he so afraid of? she wondered.

He *still* expected California to slide into the ocean, just as Mu had.

Ivy found herself shaking her head. "The ocean floor's basalt, and the mainland granite. Both igneous rock formations, yeah—but the continental plate underlying California is dense and enduring, and *light*. It's not going to slide anywhere. Or crumble. Or shatter into any pieces. Sooner believe Kansas might wing its way to Canada. Christ," she said, "you work with minerals. You know what I'm saying."

Cosmos nodded his head vigorously. "This is it," he said.

"The very core of what I wanted to say. There's a key point here. About Cayce's theory. Yes."

She ignored him and continued, warming. "A 1000-mile wide tidal wave? Absolute bullshit," she said. "I'm asking, what would happen to Japan? What about British Columbia? Alaska. Nevermind Russia. Nevermind China. Forget Indonesia. And *all* the Pacific Islands. Mexico. South America. The fact remains"—she jabbed at the tabletop with her fingernail—"an ocean can't rise up and swallow 25,000 square miles of a continent and then sink back down as if nothing happened."

She stood there, puzzling over the irises, as if next *they* might want to slide into the ocean.

"Truly fine," Cosmos said. "Excellent point," he told her.

"What *if* California started sliding into the ocean? What would you do?" She paused, as if to think of all the things one might do. And then the words burst forth. "Would you lasso it? Hold it back?" She rocked forward on the balls of her feet. "Face it, other than when some psychic claims an 8-pointer on the Richter scale is about to hit, we live as if California's permanent. We don't even think about how it might end. But you do, Cosmos. And that's my point."

"Incisive of you," he murmured. A few moments passed in silence. Ivy didn't immediately glance over at him so surprised was she; they'd argued this before—but always to different ends.

Cosmos joined his hands before him. "I think Cayce made a—let's say he misinterpreted his vision. You understand? Obviously California did not sink in '38 or '68, like he said it would." He took in a breath and fixed his eyes on her, the light-green. "I think he picked up on what happened 10,000 years ago. With Mu. I think Cayce mislead himself. Which would then mean that those entities from Mu who currently reside in California—it means nothing. They aren't going to lead California to atomic holocaust. Look, as a civilization, Mu lasted 200 centuries. Anybody could've come from Mu. We all probably did. I mean, there is that notion that it was the biblical Garden of Eden. Do you see? I mean, I feel more comfortable now." He extended his hand toward her. "You're an entity from Mu. But so what?"

Ivy kept her eyes on him. "When you talk about Mu, you really mean—."

He tilted his head a bit, as if listening to some distant call. "It," he said. "I mean Mu."

"You're not coming clean on this, Cosmos."

He stepped away from her backwards, as if she'd pushed him. "Ivy, I still want to research these ideas with you. More than that, I want to be with you. Love you. Don't let all this be an impediment. The misinterpretation. The factual bungle. I know my explanation could be improved upon, had I a more profound knowledge of the ancient. I'm sorry to say this but it's the best I can do." He smiled at her. "You can see my error," he said.

They stood close enough to touch but neither moved. "Knowledge of the ancient," she breathed.

He nodded his head once. "On Mu."

It was what they'd always had, together.

Some couples looked to the future, and the life, there, they hoped to live: a house, cars, a suburban lawn. Ivy and Cosmos turned to the past: had these two entities met during other visits to the earth plane? Were they in each other's cluster of significant entities which combine life after death after life? He'd helped her find out about her past lives, how her soul had begun on Mu. The Medium, Countess Mulberry, had entered a trance-like state and begun speaking in a voice unlike her normal waking voice. She twisted a hanky in her hands like a little girl would, and swung her feet. And talked about the entity that was Ivy.

"Comes now, in 50,000 B.C. nations gathered to combat the encroachment of enormous beasts, and the creeping things of the earth," she murmured. "Your soul then was among those of that group from Lemuria who gathered to subdue the earth." Ivy listened as if hypnotized, there in the cramped parlor, staring up at the tapestries hung over the walls, and all the silk cloths draped about. They enchanted her, the fables of Mu and her part in them; beside her, Cosmos occasionally nodded his head to what Countess Mulberry said.

And what a way to get to know someone—by going through the long-gone, mythical past! It was like a new act of intimacy they alone had created.

For his own part, Cosmos liked to tell her bedtime stories of Mu. "When I talk in my sleep," he said, "I speak the language of Mu. And when I dream," he said, "that's where I go." He made it all quite fantastical, lyrical—and she was happy to join in.

"I was a Mumaid," she said. "Queen of the Mumaids. I wore a crown and had a head of luxurious, thick hair intermingled with strands of pure 24k gold."

One night, after turning out the lights, she was just about to doze off, when he said, "You remember the sea monkeys they used to advertise in the backs of Marvel comic books? They come from Mu. And you know that crabmeat substitute called Sea Legs? It's made from the sea monkey when it becomes too elderly to be of use to its society any longer." He grew drowsier; his voice seemed to come a great distance. Ivy listened to his breathing grow deeper, slower. "There's more phosphorous in Sea Legs than in any other food item. And you know the more gold in your blood, the better." It was as if he'd mesmerized himself and now spoke to her. "Think about the dessicated shrimps," he whispered into her hair what seemed several minutes later. "The ones you find in a styrofoam bowl of Maruchan noodles—you know, just before you pour the boiling water in. Those shrimps once thrived there. And the lobsters of Mu are so civilized people don't eat them. They want to learn from them, instead. How they choose their mates, for instance." Here, he became more alert and spoke to her as if giving a lesson. "When she's ready to molt, the woman walks to where the man lives and leaves her scent outside his door. Then the man opens his door and invites her in. She begins to remove her hard, protective covering, to reveal all her vulnerability and trust him. This turns the man on." He licked his lips, and there was a moment. "When she stands clothed only in her softness before him, he takes her in his arms and makes love to her with a gentleness that is almost human. Afterward, the woman lives with the man for several days, until her shell covers her again. And they part." Cosmos now seemed fully awake. "They part, but they'll make love again. They will make love the rest of their lives. Only with each other."

After a few moments she said. "Mu."

The pillowcase crackled as he nodded against it. "That's right," he said.

She hugged closer to Cosmos. "Cows say moo," she told him.

"Ooooooooooooooooo," he said. "And sometimes they leap over the mooooooooooooooooooon."

But he was a restless sleeper. He tossed and flopped about. Whistled through his nose. She could hear him grinding his teeth. Even when dreaming he didn't seem at rest.

"You're an old soul," he'd said once—out of nowhere. "You've been around."

They were standing in her kitchen, an open box of take-out pizza between them, mozzarella rapidly hardening on the cardboard.

"How can you be so certain?"

He'd lifted a too-hot slice to his mouth and now dropped it back in the box. Black olives scattered. "Because you're nearly vegetarian," he said, and pointed to a small pile of sausage she'd picked from her pizza.

Whatever she'd done in prior incarnations was unavailable to him, as *fact*. He could listen to Countess Mulberry, and research the history of Lemuria and draw his own conclusions, but he couldn't know for certain things like how she'd lived—the quality of her life—and when. Or with whom she'd slept.

Cosmos' necklace sparkled out at Ivy now—all that silver, and the stones. Didn't it get heavy? Her hand went instinctively to her breastbone and the ruby, its angles hard enough to cut. Twice it had tried to leap.

What did leaping mean?

Because both times when the chain broke it felt like cool water trickling across her skin.

"I haven't slept with some other man," Ivy said. Neither budged; their utter stillness made her feel encased by the room and the heady, sweet scent which semed shot through everything. "But if I had, what could you do about it?" She watched him. "Tie me up? Chain me down?"

Cosmos threw his head back, and she saw a deep blush spread from his cheeks down his neck. When he spoke a moment later, his stammer assured her she'd touched a tender spot. "This is the thing I bungled," he told her. "It was my mistake. My problem."

She heard herself swallow.

A couple months back they had lain in her bed one morning, talking. "In my dreams I see the entity that is you rise up from your body," he had said, "the gleaming silver cord attached umbilically. A cloud of electric green light envelops you. Deep green. Green of the Regina red wine vinegar bottle. With hints of navy blue. Like the green flash that appears on the ocean just as the sun sinks underneath. I can see the shining cord twisting within it." He had stopped then. "You know about the gleaming silver cord, don't you?"

Ivy nestled deeper into the sheets, near him. She shook her head.

"It links your soul to the physical body. When the gleaming cord is severed, you die." He leaned up on his elbow to look at her. "Oh, don't worry. It's always been intact for you."

That was when she still felt she slept free.

"What really are you afraid of?" she asked him now.

Without turning his head, he lifted his gaze; it seemed the tint of his eyes, that animate color, had moved under its own power.

A moment passed.

She'd seen the body without the protection life provided, and she'd lived through that astonishment, other rarities, too, some unspeakable. It scared her. Nothing had changed that. Lying naked and lifeless there, the body still retained all its mystery—it hoarded it, sealed it up in an irascible stillness. She had seen it, she had gazed into eyes forever lidded at half-mast; in five minutes she knew she'd be back in the laboratory, *with it,* working her magic, correcting death. All she did was *beautify* it, after all; she didn't *know.* And that had prepared her for little, certainly not for the darkness of love's dying. The sensation hung in her bosom like a rock her hands could not dislodge. She picked up the planter of irises and held it out to him.

"Ivy...," he whispered

"It's alive," she said. "And it wants to goddamn stay that way."

A lock of hair fell over his forehead; she could tell his teeth were tightly clenched. When he looked at her, it was with wild eyes. *"Alive,"* he said. "What do you know about it? I'll always think you sabotaged that cactus. And killed James, goddammit. What parakeet dies?" he cried. "Yeah, you work with *dead* things all the time. Your job takes you *far* from life! Look at this!" and he gestured about at the room, its immaculate carpet, its tables for flowers, all the emptiness which tomorrow would hold someone else's suffering and grief. I'm surprised you even know how to act around people. Oh, Jesus Christ," he said. A paroxysm seemed to pass through every muscle in his body.

But after a moment he took the planter she held.

And her arms felt light, as if they might drift up toward the ceiling, instead of falling to rest at her sides.

She *did* work with people.

Even alone at Orange Coast Mortuary, she was still working with people. People after the struggle for life ends. After the surrender. Ivy knew things about the living, just as she knew things about the dead—and enough about both to know that most people were wrong about the change called death. It was so clean, for one thing. Even the stillness, she felt, was misunderstood. The handful of times she'd worked in the embalming room alone, the click of her heels on the tile floor seemed embedded in a cottony silence, a thick, cushiony one you'd choose for storing precious things.

Dying in the Goldenwest

"**A** woman was pecked to death down at Balboa Pier by frenzied gulls while jogging," Bobby Lu said, reading from the newspaper spread on the picnic table before her. "A man was playing chicken with the widebodies at LAX and was mutilated. They found his legs 200 yards down the runway. At Zuma a youth hit his head on a surf board and drowned. Here's where they found some woman's severed hand. The right hand," she said and pointed to a haywire line-drawing of where the Artesia and Cypress Grove freeways joined at Hawaiian Gardens. "Such peaceful names, too," she murmured. "What's going on?" She riffled the pages of the newspaper. "The word 'grisly' has been used five times already. Doesn't some old lady somewhere out weeding her pansies stand up, suddenly clutch at her heart, and then keel over? Won't that ever happen? Or do I have to go back home to get the soft-core news?" She bent over the paper, stabbing her finger at a small column with a large block headline. "An adolescent was fished from the San Gabriel River, his wrists chained to his ankles, cigarette burns on his nipples. Jesus, are there only public deaths out there?"

Emily was sitting neck-deep in the hot tub, her head resting back on a wadded up towel. Steeping, she thought, watching the water churn and swirl, as if boiling, around her. She glanced across the patio. Bobby Lu had black newsprint shadows on either elbow; she'd been making her study most the morning. "That's just the SANTA ANA REGISTER," Emily said. Sweat rolled down the sides of her face. "It reports sensationalistic news items."

Bobby Lu snorted. "You're saying maybe some other paper *suppresses* them? That someone's *keeping* them from us?"

Emily shrugged her shoulders to ease the tightness there. "Oh, no," she said. "Never from us. We'll know all, by God." And she popped her fist up out of the water for emphasis. Plumes of steam rose from her skin and then faded off into the air. Bobby Lu had arrived yesterday with Nick's older brother C.A., in the new car he'd bought her for quitting smoking. They'd driven throughout most of the Southwest— the odometer already registered over 2000 miles—and then parked the car in Santa Ana, in Emily and Nick's driveway, deciding to drop in and spend a few days with them. C.A. had walked in bearing gifts: he set a 10 pound sack of black popcorn down on the kitchen counter, a half-case of barbecued mutton from the On-Time Bar-B-Q in their old neighborhood next to it, and then stacked up two six-packs of Stroh's—

all things you couldn't buy in California. "I feel like a smuggler," he had said, rolling his pants leg up and pulling from inside his boot a clear glass flask full of ugly, teeming water. "Lake Michigan," he'd said, suspending the flask between two fingers as if it were a bell. A wadded gum wrapper floated in it, for authenticity—but Emily recognized it as the fruity brand C.A. always chewed. He'd held the flask close to her ear and swished it. "Mag Mile," he whispered. "The Gold Coast," he said.

Later, Bobby Lu had helped her with dinner. Emily was at the butcher block, chopping apples for a Waldorf salad. "C.A. says I should carry this around with me. Like a good-luck charm," Bobby Lu had said. She'd pulled a crumpled, filthy cigarette butt from her shirt pocket. "I'm supposed to take it out and smell it every time I feel like smoking. And I do," she said. She pressed it to her nose. "It smells so good."

Emily's own cigarette lay burning on the rim of the sink, and she wondered if, as a courtesy, she should stub it out. C.A.'s cackle sounded from the living room; he laughed high-pitched, like a woman crying out in danger. "You need a hobby," Emily had said, after she took a long drag and exhaled slowly. "And you shouldn't carry that nasty thing around with you either."

"It's my willpower," Bobby Lu said, handling it. "Or C.A. thinks it is. I *had* to quit, Emily. You don't know what it's like. I was *killing* myself. And him too. *He* got *nodes*. On his larynx." She ate an apple chunk and said, "Diversions, though—you're absolutely right on that point, you know it? I need some diversion. A friend of mine said she relied on Amanda York novels and Irish Mist when she quit smoking. Later, when she went on the wagon, she turned to Ross McDonald and Hostess Ho-Ho's. She said she felt guilty but that it worked. Of course, now she weighs 190 pounds, but the thing is," Bobby Lu said, "the thing is, I don't read bodice-rippers or whodunnits. And I don't want to paint by numbers either, or attend ceramics classes in the afternoon. I don't have any pleasures I can feel guilty *about*. But I need one. I can see that clearly. I need just one," she said. She tapped her fingers on the chopping block. "Maybe you'll give me one of yours."

Emily scraped apple seeds from her hands. "Mine?" she said.

"Oh, don't be coy," she said. "Now, which would you give up?"

"I'm not aware of having any."

Bobby Lu chuckled. "Well, Nick seems to think you do. I

talk to Nick sometimes," she said. "Really talk. He shares his life with me."

Emily wiped her hands on a towel. "If I have any sinful pleasures, I haven't noticed they've helped any." She picked her cigarette up from the edge of the sink and took a drag, a case in point.

Bobby Lu folded her arms across her chest and leaned back. "She doesn't say yes, she doesn't say no. Interesting. Emily's evasive these days. See, Nick tells me that, too."

"Since when is my life any of your business?"

But Bobby Lu was eyeing her cigarette, entranced. "You know, some people quit and find out they aren't *really* smokers. Not *born* smokers. But I *am*. I found myself standing before a cigarette machine as if it were an altar." She looked up. "At Gilbert Ortega's in Flagstaff, Arizona. Let me take a puff," she said. She tucked the smelly cigarette butt back in her shirt pocket and smiled. "I can't resist," she said. "Come on."

"What about that new car in the driveway? C.A. thinks you've quit," Emily said, cigarette poised between them. "What about his larynx?"

"Shhhhhhhhh," Bobby Lu said. She slid her fingers among Emily's and extracted the cigarette from them. She puffed and swayed back, as if giddy on the smoke. "I've quit," she said. "Oh, I have. But I just need one. Just this one." She sneaked another tiny one and left a smear of lipstick on the filter.

"What a mess you are!" Emily said.

Bobby Lu shrugged. "C.A. won't notice, so he needn't know." She took out a Binaca and aimed the nozzle at the back of her mouth. There was a hiss. "One spray and it's like it never happened. Oh, there *are* easier things to cover up. But not everything is this easy." She sprayed the nozzle again.

"Being married to him has finally robbed you of all subtlety. What is it here? What does Bobby Lu think she knows?"

"Only that I talk to Nick, Emily. He tells me he worries sometimes."

It was as if those words had invaded her body, and then even the salad she was making. At dinner it tasted off. Later that night, when she reached far back in her dresser drawer for her carton of cigarettes, she noticed a couple packs missing. She stared at the drawer. It was her private place. She kept her underwear there!

Now heat rose from the water in shimmering coils; sweat dripped from Emily's hairline. Nothing had faded, had passed on since then; though Bobby Lu's curiosity had waned and then gone altogether, none of the discomfort it had aroused, that which she still felt, had died. "Don't be overly-familiar," was how she'd ended their chat yesterday in the kitchen. But the sense of having been invaded smoldered within her. Emily stared across the patio. Bobby Lu still sat puzzling over the news. "When people die back home," she was saying "it's soft and quiet. Death isn't gruesome. It's like it sounds! Easeful. Homey. It's what's going to happen to all of us."

Emily blinked down at the water, her skin golden just beneath; the color seemed to undulate in voluptuous waves. Gacy's asphalt-covered backyard immediately sprang to mind, as did the image of a woman hanging from her heels, decapitated, gutted like a deer, in a barn in Wisconsin. What happens discreetly Back East is enough to shame the devil, she thought, and smashed her arm out across the water, as if to clear her sight.

"Yeah, a lot of people say they'll never come to California. The land of fruits and nuts," Bobby Lu added in a low voice.

What about dates, little mess? Are they fruits? They grow on trees. Okay—they grow on *palm* trees, but are they fruits or are they not? And Emily's heart began to pound as she saw herself making her point, ramming dates sideways down Bobby Lu's throat, and then coconuts, because coconuts grew on trees, too, and they might also be fruits.

"In Leisure World, at Laguna Niguel, a spinster was run down by a golf cart driven by an ...," Bobby Lu began, but the front door banged and after a moment C.A. filled the patio doorway, Nick lagging behind. He spread a broad hand before him and began counting on his fingers. "I love my computer. I love my dog. I share the road with runners. I've hugged my kids today and even my horse. I know that if I can read this I'm either too close or I should thank some teacher. I think the U.S. should get out of El Salvador." He rolled his eyes elaborately. "Jesus, driving the freeways," he said.

"You mean you *heart* your computer," Emily said.

He glanced down at her. "I mean I'm sick of reading the ass-end of everybody's car. I'm sure I sound like the ugly American, here in California, but this is ersatz. There's too much self-promotion. It's a fool's paradise," he said.

Nick laughed. "Well, that's the cliche. We'll show you the romantic side—how it really is. The state's nickname in Spanish is *El Estado del Oro*, for instance. You know, for all the sunshine and oranges and blonde-folk, and the prospecting."

"Gold?" C.A. said. "Gold*brick,* you mean." He had a Knott's Berry Farm t-shirt draped over his shoulder and a souvenir pamphlet from the Movieland Wax Museum tucked under his arm. "Yeah, I'm not having any. It shan't suck me in," he said. "No." Just then Nick snatched the t-shirt and shook it out before him.

"Oh, you're six feet above contradiction, aren't you?"

C.A. blushed a deep wine and, cackling, opened his arms, as if throwing off all disguise. The pamphlet dropped like a felled bird to the concrete.

He always wore a sock hat because he was going bald.

When she set the snapper down on the dinner table, Emily looked at C.A.'s hat—the upturned cuff and ribbed knit, the wooly ball like a motionless explosion at his crown. It was only a hat, and it made him look goddamn silly, but something lay concealed just beneath, a process mysterious and irrevocable that worked in secret, in silence. Without intending to, Emily edged around him. And as she passed behind his chair, the urge to yank the hat up off his head shook her hand. Nick caught her eye from across the table and he blinked twice, as if wondering about her attention to the hat. He had olive-colored eyes and the most beautifully shaped mouth she'd ever seen—a fair, bronze-haired man, thirty-one, going soft at the waist and hips, yet boyishly so. Emily looked from him to C.A.'s hat, and then away.

As she passed the salad to Bobby Lu, the phone rang, and she ran to the kitchen to answer it.

Roy's voice startled her.

"I've got a bucket, and I've got a plastic shovel. I'm going to take you pismoing!"

She laughed. "I almost bought pismos yesterday, at the market."

"Oh, don't do that," he said. "Don't ever do that. They probably sit there all the live-long day. Listen," he said, "we can sneak down to the beach at midnight—no, we'll *steal* down to the beach—and dig up a hundred clams. 'Tis the season, babe. They'll only be good a few days."

She said, "Oh God Almighty, this is cruel," and told him about her house-guests. "I can't get away—not today, not even tomorrow!"

Roy's sigh made a tinny sound over the line, like a child's wind-up toy. She heard Nick in the hall and said into the receiver, "Well, Roy he's right here. Let me get him for you."

Roy chuckled. "Nick!" he said. "Ma'am, I don't want *Nick*. I want *you*."

Exhilarated, Emily handed the phone to Nick, who said, "C.A. needs the tartar sauce" and then, turning, "What the hell's up?" into the mouthpiece.

She rummaged around among shadowy containers in the refrigerator and listened to him explain something about an upcoming project; both he and Roy worked for Western Digital. After he had hung up, he looked at her, worry-creases around his eyes. "What's wrong?" he said.

She shook her head. "How do you mean?"

"Are they driving you crazy?"

She nodded. "But no worse than usual."

Nick exhaled slowly, as if clearing his lungs. He stared at the tartar sauce, then the phone. As Emily headed toward the doorway, she saw him reach over and unclip the phone from its jack.

"The Volkswagens travel alongside the Alfa Romeos here, and everyone's got something to advertise," C.A. said when she came back in the room. "I want to scream, 'Look, I've got to *drive* the stretch of road *behind* you—I don't want to get *intimately* involved!' " His gaze rested on her. "*Can* you go any place here for a quiet moment? I feel crowded in my own skin!"

Emily slipped her napkin on her lap. "California's really a bucket of feathers to you, isn't it?"

"Well, it's pretty and so forth—but I'm not impressed by all the self-advertisement, and stuff."

"And stuff?" Nick said, taking his seat.

"I don't need any of that."

Bobby Lu speared some snapper. "Only a hat," she said.

He turned to her. "Yes, my dear. And what about my hat?"

"Folks, just to set the record straight, he doesn't sleep in the hat."

"I'm embarrassed." C.A. said, glancing down at his plate. "Is that what you want, Lu?" He broke into a big smile. "Now I'm embarrassed."

Nick winked at Bobby Lu. "It's a Charles Anthony original."

C.A. eyed him. "Don't laugh too hard, bro, because it's going to happen to you. And you can take that to the bank," he said. "Right? Pop's mother was bald, or something like that. Am I right?" He gazed dazedly out the window. "The women, partner. If they don't get you here"—he cupped his crotch—"they get you here." He pointed to his head.

Nick sipped a Stroh's. "Well, when it happens, I'm not going to camouflage it." As C.A. looked up, puzzled, Nick nodded at the hat. "Camouflage it."

C.A. said, "This isn't camouflage. It's too obvious to be camouflage. If I painted my scalp turquoise it couldn't be more obvious."

"So, then, what's the point, is, I think, what Nick means," Bobby Lu said.

"Point?" C.A. said. "There is no point!"

He plucked it off his head and flung his arms back, the sock hat flying across the dining area to the living room. What hair he had was reddish-gold, like Nick's and stood on end. The hat snagged the corner of an old framed photo of Emily and Nick taken just before their wedding, and it hung there.

Emily stared into the living room.

The photo had stood in its sleek, ultra-modern frame on the formica end table for four years—she had picked it up and dusted it off a hundred times—but that hat now made all the difference; she stared as if anew. Not at *it*, but at the boy and girl in the picture. They stood before the Frank Lloyd Wright house which looks like a boat, back at the U of C, their pre-California skin pasty-looking, winter having leached all color from it. She had changed since then in small yet astoundingly visible ways. And *he* had changed. That grinning, long-haired boy who stood staring confidently over his shoulder at the camera conveyed a cellular change, an aural one. The difference between that boy and Nick—both lovely, and handsome men—but that palpable difference...! His hair color was a shade lighter now, more like hers, and it had the curl hers did. It was as if the planes of his face had smoothed out, since Chicago, became angular, like hers. Could that happen, the constancy of matrimony gradually filing away his features, like wind sculpting sand? The floor seemed to tilt under her.

Then C.A. snatched his sock hat from the picture frame.

He stared at her and at the photo. "You'll never look that good again," he said. "Either one of you." He slapped his hand once on the table, laughing.

That night as she showered, Nick came in the bathroom, and she watched through the half-clear, half-frosted pattern in the vinyl shower curtain as he unbuttoned his shirt, hung it up on the doorknob, getting ready for bed. He shimmied out of his jeans, and over the hiss of water said, "I was hoping we could buy some pismo clams while C.A. and Bobby Lu were visiting."

Emily stood breathless.

Nick wiped away a little smear of steam from the shower curtain. "Hello?" he said. He poked his head in, and Emily peered up from under the ragged fringe of her bangs. He said, "An underground pipe burst and is spilling raw sewage into Emerald Bay. They've quarantined the beach for a week."

Her heart seemed to flip. She imagined it flipping visibly, bulging between her breasts.

"Well, don't look so worried," he told her. "We'll think of something else." He leaned back out of the shower and she watched through the vinyl as he peeled his briefs down and kicked out of them. He was pretty, anyone could see, just as he always had been. Any changes about him had to do with *her:* with smothering in ease and privity. Being laid open by love. Dead of promiscuity. She did not regard this last in the usual sexual sense, not a promiscuous abandoning of the self to many, but, *solo,* each to the other: that Emily and Nick be *one,* not two—slaughtering their solitude in order to join whatever parts lay dismembered in its wake. Married people begin to resemble each other for a good reason, she thought, remembering the photo: life lived in so abject a commutuality left hardly any membrane between *her* cells and *his.* She needed a private place, *in vitrio,* a roped off spot in her heart that only she could jealously possess. And some way to hide it.

C.A.'s sock hat came to mind. If she were him, and it were *her* secret, she'd never take the goddamn thing off, not to make love or go to the bathroom or swim to save her life. Thought of it made her smile.

Nick slid the curtain on its hooks and stepped in next to her. He rubbed his hands along her ribs, his grin a white slice. Sometimes she thought he knew, sometimes not—and she wondered if it mattered, what it did to him, what he suffered. Did he act differently toward her, did he, for instance, move his hand up the slope of her breast now, tug at the nipple, to keep the pressure there?

Water sparkled silver in his hair.

She was surviving the mystery of love's dying.

"I like it when you smile," he said.

Sunlight rippled on the surface of San Joaquin Bay like a path of hammered gold you could walk right across into another world. Roy's bungalow lay just beyond the harbor bridge, just as far west as she could go without driving into the Pacific; her tires hummed on the bridge as she crossed over.

Bobby Lu, C.A., Nick and Emily had all planned to sail out to Catalina this morning and spend the day there—take a picnic lunch, lots of film, make a day of it. But she had begged off, claiming she'd lost a contact lens and would have to make a trip to the optometrist's. Bobby Lu now smoked Emily's cigarettes openly, and *C.A.* had developed a hacking cough—but the two had decided to go to Catalina anyway. They bumped around the kitchen, hardly speaking, smearing bread with mayonnaise and slapping down cold cuts for sandwiches. Nick had stared wordlessly after Emily as she went to the door, as she paused there, the color high in her cheeks, trying to remember everything—checkbook, contact lens case—too excited to care if he did suspect anything, to care about his silent attention. He followed her out to the drive, stopping next to his car as she got into hers. In her last glimpse of him as she pulled away, he was still standing there, his hand resting on one fender.

At Roy's she waited on the porch several moments for him to answer the door. There seemed a dead calm throughout the upper bay, scarcely breeze enough to stir the eucalyptus leaves. All the sunfish and starfish and catamarans and sloops in the harbor seemed fixed to the water, as if glued, their shrouds hanging noiseless. His bungalow was old and tiny; yellow paint peeled away from the wood in long curls. Squat marigolds grew among the encroaching dandelions, the sun full on them now, making them unusually golden. The porch and the banister on the porch were painted a thick, industrial-strength maize. The banister was chipped in places, revealing long, rusty scabs. Roy's place was in disarray, falling apart— shutters hanging, floorboards which creaked; it seemed any slight wind could dismantle it.

He opened the door in his shorts, his hair flat on one side from sleep. His blue eyes widened; he appeared keyed-up, she thought, or surprised. Surprised to see her. Emily liked to surprise him, she liked to be silly with him. Once, for his birthday she'd filled his bathroom with balloons. He'd been delighted, had bounded into the room—balloons flying up and shrieking as their taut skins rubbed—as if he were smashing through surf. And the sun streaming through that roomful

of color had thrown such a peculiar light on his face. He'd
not had the heart to pop any of them—"I can't *murder*
them," he'd said. Even a week later a dozen slowly-shriveled
balloons still lay about, occasionally bumping at her ankles.
That was last February; things had been right at Roy's.

Now Emily pushed past him, laughing, and went down
the hall, teasing her dress from her shoulders and hips as she
did, letting it fall in a heap of blue. His windows were covered
with foil and heavily shaded, in order to keep the house cool,
and from inside she always misguessed, thought it was rain-
ing or dark outside when it was not. It seemed a place of the
utmost privacy. When people talked about digging a hole and
crawling into it in order to elude the world she knew this was
what they meant; Roy offered her refreshment and escape.
Today, it looked like night inside his house; when she yanked
the curtain cord, sunlight sliced golden across the floor. She
got into his bed like she'd done it for years and would all the
rest of her days. Could she give up the ghost here, remnants of
that old life dying away as she pulled back the quilt and
slipped under the covers—the last of it gone with her cries?
She'd heard that the eyes of a dead woman can live again, can
open fresh on a world that is young. Could Emily, in rising,
begin anew? Roy normally slept with both pillows on his side
of the bed; now, they lay side by side. It seemed he'd been
expecting *her*. Her heart beat faster.

"Hey," he said, from the hallway.

"Come quick," she said. She passed her hands over her
body, as if to feel skin for the first time. "I know what I want.
I've made up my mind." Roy's rabbit—Bill—hopped into
the bedroom and regarded her with his flashy yellow eyes. His
toe nails clicked on the bare wood floor. The rabbit thumped
down in the corner and sighed. He looked up at her as if to
say, "I'm glad you are here."

Roy said, "Jesus, I didn't know you were coming."

She waited for more, his hesitation so unusual.

"Kill me," he said, "Good Christ, take me now. Oh, this is
bad."

Emily leapt up off the mattress as if it'd burned her. She
listened into the cool dark of his house. The stillness of her
own neighborhood was familiar—and natural since she lived
at the apex of a quiet cul de sac—but she had no precedent for
it here, not amid memories of his breath at her ear, the wet
sounds their bodies made, and what they'd moaned. That had
always muted the world, and whatever life, for her, might
exist outside, full of its complexities and sadness. Now the

quiet was mystery itself, hard to focus on for more than a few seconds. Instead, she listened to her blood pulsing along, the real sounds of her body working, living.

When she got to the kitchen, she saw Roy and a young blonde woman who sat at the kitchen table in one of his button-down shirts. He had his hands up around his face, transfixed, as if before a disaster. The woman stared down at the table, not looking up. Her hair feathered back in full, wispy layers—like yellow smoke. She was stunning and younger than Emily.

"Tell me she's your sister," Emily heard herself saying. The kitchen curtains billowed out on what seemed the first breeze of the day, and street noises filtered in: the chirr of a kid's Big Wheel on the pavement, a lawnmower somewhere. Sounds of people going about life. And gulls—! She heard them as if for the first time. The humming sound of a car drawing closer also wafted in from the street, mixing with a radio in the distance and the few shrouds that clanked in the harbor below. At first she thought the car had pulled into a neighbor's drive, but then she heard the crunch of gravel, the engine noise near.

Roy slumped heavily on the step ladder. "Not in my wild-est dreams did I imagine you'd stop by today." He looked around. Neither looked at the woman. Emily listened to the steady engine throb outside his house, the gulls and other sounds of harbor life all muffled by it. Then the car peeled out. The winding of gears faded down the street, and after several moments an acrid, rubber smell came in through the window, dying away under her nose.

"Is she your wife? Or who?" the woman asked, the ques-tions so deliberate she held her hand over the table, thrusting first one finger out, then another.

Roy was still shaken. "Oh, this is bad," he said.

Emily began backing toward the door. "I didn't call before coming over," she mumbled. Her dress lay in the hall like cast off skin. She stooped and lifted it. Standing just out of view of the kitchen, she slid into it, smoothed it down over her hips.

"Wait, Emily," Roy said as she went to the door.

He followed her outside where the sun dazzled, seemed to bleach all color from the sky. She shielded her eyes against the light, blinded for the moment, his house such a sanctuary of shade. She would've expected thunderheads, or night-time, anything dark, not sharp tree shadows etched across his lawn and the lawns of neighboring houses. Even the squat marigolds threw shadows that were clean at the edges. After only a moment, though, it all began to shimmer before her eyes.

"Now, come on," Roy said. "None of that." He reached forward to wipe her cheek.

Emily jerked her arms up over her head, then slammed them hard against his chest. "Bastard!" she cried.

Roy held her fists, even after she no longer struggled. He said, "Emily, what is it you expect here? You *barge* in. Unannounced! This is my life," he said. "It's *mine*." And he tightened his hands around hers with all the fervor of possession. "I'm glad you're in it, don't get me wrong, and I don't mean this to sound unkind—but you're not all of it. Come on, Emily, you know what I'm saying. You still sleep with Nick."

Her eyes darted from him to the street, the pavement lying silver in the uncompromising sun, its skidmarks like a newly blazed trail that would take her back to Nick and whatever he knew. The breath rattled in her throat. "Yeah," she said.

Roy slid his arms around her with the care one takes in handling too hot objects. She felt his lips against her hair. "Oh," he moaned. " 'Tis airy nothing, my dear. What you see here. All of it." His hands rubbed along her back.

"Everything?" she asked after a bit.

Without pulling away, Roy said, "Honey, you have Nick. And it's good"—he shifted against her—"that you do."

Heat spread, as if animate, across her body. She'd read of spontaneous combustion and public self-immolation and innocent children doused with gasoline and set afire by thugs—this wasn't like any of it. A wildfire roared beneath her skin, reaming the veins with a white-hot blaze, leaping from one vein to another as brushfires leap freeways. She began to collapse under the sensation. Land was not land—it all passed away beneath her. Life seemed to give up its gold. The color of Roy's place was like something she'd dreamed, and it began to fade.

A man mowing grass had stopped to look her way. Two boys, skateboards in tow, leaned against a tall palm, watching. Even the young blonde woman stood, Emily imagined in her torment, at the kitchen window, the better to see.

She clung to Roy, as to life, and, mouth open, gasped the air. Hard breaths carved that passageway—her respiratory tract—as if for the first time.

The Green Life

"**I** can't compete with him," Hanes said.

"Who?"

He leaned across the table and tapped her temple. "Him up here."

They were at El Zocalo, one-time adobe tract house turned restaurant—she could still imagine where the sofa might stand, where the TV would go—and she was staring down at her platter of cod Veracruz; there had been a lull in the conversation before he spoke, a silence filled by her glancing about at a younger couple who cuddled in a corner booth, and his dragging a tortilla chip across the creamy surface of the frijoles, the chip snapping half-way through. "He clings like a scallop, doesn't he? The man in your mind."

She smiled lamely. "I thought you were going to say the man in the moon."

Hanes seemed either to growl or snort, the noise settling uneasily among the clink of forks, the click of ice cubes in water glasses around them. "He may as well be the man in the moon, for all the good he does you here. On earth. Among us." When she glanced up, he said, "The living."

Maizie half-flinched at that, like a sleeper awakened. "He's alive."

As Hanes turned his blue eyes on her, she felt something like a droplet of icy water trickle down her spine. "But not for you," he said. With that, he reached over, speared some cod from her plate, and popped it in his mouth with the possessive air of a child winning an argument.

She picked up the tab that evening, too much the possessive child herself to let that go, and after driving Hanes home—15 minutes of stop lights and a thick, iced silence—she got on the Garden Grove, exiting at Bolsa Chica, intending to drive past Lee Greencastle's. She loved everything about the approach: how the streets wound deeper and deeper in on themselves, his home nestled at the center, the very cordium of his neighborhood. It was just after sunset, and a lot of underground sprinkler systems were watering: the only time, in summer, it was safe to do that without fear of burning the lawn in the relentless California sun.

The water jets looked like spun silver in her headlights.

His sprinklers *weren't* turned on, but she saw his house through the mist of other yards as she edged down the block. It was a tabby house, like those she'd once seen set, row after row, far off the beaches of the Florida coast, their exteriors a sturdy mix of mortar and crushed oyster shell. Only his house stood in Cathedral City—and the shells weren't oysters but the soft, chalky ones of vertebrae that had been dredged from the bottom of the San Gabriel River, shells that were still delicate so that even now if you brushed up against the house you would come away with a faint powdery trace on your skin or clothing. One ragged palm stood in his yard, its fronds so dry they made a wild, thrashing sound when the wind blew.

She stopped in the middle of the street and stared. Though the windows were dark, the house radiated a pale, coolish sheen. Its white sides cast a clean light under the streetlamps, glowing like a second moon. All was calm. In the gathering shadows, the house seemed tomblike, invincible, a place she, as a girl, would've hurried past, whistling. And uncompromisingly white. She supposed embedded as it was among all the usual frame tract homes with their expected shake roofs and breaks of bougainvillea and the dental clinics, the law offices, the realtors, it did look homely. But she had felt alive there and could no longer look at it through eyes which did not see its beauty. Memory of all that made her smile, her own skin strangely illuminated, almost pearly, in the light his house reflected. Several moments had passed when, as she sat there, a faint golden glow, as from a candle, caught her eye. It illuminated the rear upstairs window, the room she remembered as his bedroom, with a fuzzy light. She knew exactly how that room looked by candlelight, his dark sheets exerting a gravitational pull so strong they could absorb light, lint, cracker crumbs, suck her in, too. She knew the walls, knew the furniture, the heavily lacquered oriental sort he'd chosen, knew how the candle's flame would reflect on the surface of the headboard, as if burning within. Could knowledge set her free? No, knowing this held her captive.

Idling in neutral, she crossed her hands over the steering wheel and lowered her forehead to her knuckles and remained in that position for some time.

She had made, of his house, a shining marble temple whose slick, cool sides cast a white brilliance from atop an enormous vista. In it, they'd lived out her dream of devotion, love and possession—the walls a foot thick, the windows of a heavy paned quartz which, by day scattered tiny rainbows all about and broke the moonlight into a thousand stars by night. She cherished this dream, protected it, saved it for rainy days when she, all alone, could fix the temple before her eyes, concerned about its rafters and the slats under its kitchen floor and insulation and yardwork, just like any other homeowner. Ocean surf exploded 100 feet below—or, sometimes, she focussed on desert winds whipping sandspouts at the door, the landscape, torched and blackened as if by runaway brushfires, incapable of supporting any life.

Because she'd been in Lee's bed only once.

Once, and even then not for an entire night—but she could imagine the *L.A. Times* there, or puppies, or eating a kiwi fruit, or wrestling with him all across the smooth flat surface that seemed a world with its own solitary dark horizon; she could imagine falling in love. Though she had never, as his lover, sat across from him in a restaurant, or gone to the grocery store, or played bingo or pitch 'n catch or gone skiing with him, what those things would be like no longer wavered, indistinct, under depths of murky water: all had been stranded along the shore as after a high-tide. They stood out like jewels in mud. She *had* sat across many restaurant tables from him, *had* gone to the grocery store and done dozens of things, both exceptional and banal, with him; and, because they were friends—good friends, but *just* friends— she could still look forward to other such experiences.

They'd shared so much already—didn't it sometimes seem they'd shared it all?

No matter in which part of the Southland she found herself, no matter how securely locked in her own apartment, the temple squatted clearly within view. She understood its invitation to cast her life, anew, exactly in the mold of her old life, and gave herself to it, her very own torment.

When after several minutes she lifted her head, it was to wild swatches of blue light washing over her, an Orange County police car just behind. She unrolled her window as an officer approached. "I was looking for an address," she stammered.

He asked for her license, bending so close she could smell his sweet, minty breath; she realized he no doubt wanted to smell *hers,* as a preliminary measure of sobriety. The officer straightened and sauntered around her car. "Your left headlight is out," he told her, stooping again alongside the window. "Let me hear you say you'll promptly get it fixed."

Mumbling her assent, she slid her license back into her wallet.

She drove all the way home with a pounding heart.

There was too much Maizie didn't know about the human body.

Why hers was keeping her awake nights, as if under her skin squawked an infant on a bad schedule. Why his had seemed warmer than any other man's. Was that possible? She groaned and rolled over, twisting herself deeper in the sheets. After 20 minutes more, she untangled herself, stumbled over toward the shoulder-high bedroom window. There were 452 units in her complex; she knew for a fact her particular floor-plan repeated itself 289 times throughout Hampton Square. How many other tenants stood similarly, arms crossed on the window sill, chin resting on hands, staring out at the carport? Nothing seemed more lonely than its pebbly roof stretching unbroken across the complex for a full eighth of a mile, like some strip of barren desert, a place her thoughts could wander lost. Lee often told her she knew him better than anyone and for that reason said she could help out with his troubles. They went back three years together, to Pepperdine, where she remembered being troubled by nothing more than cranky professors, too much sun, poor surf. Later, they were both troubled in the job market, he finally ending up before a computer terminal, she guiding tours at Living World Marina. Still later, her troubles concerned his house: help first with his deciding to buy it. He had come into some money upon his uncle's death, money which he frittered for six months—he was really blowing the whole wad. On a whim, California real estate looked good, just as floating a party of people out to Catalina the week before had "looked good," or Palm Desert for brunch, Ensenada at midday, Squaw Valley for sunset had. And there, for his whimsy, sat the tabby house; he had just enough to put down and cover closing. After, rainspouts needed to be cleared, there were ice plants to tend, supports under the kitchen floor to check; together they had replaced broken ceramic roof tiles, substituting dusky, twice-fired blue ones for the unglazed terra cotta so that his roof now appeared variegated, like a cob of Indian corn. She had helped him remove dead fronds from the palm so that it no longer represented a fire hazard.

And singlehandedly spackled every earthquake crack in the walls.

How many tremors had they had since then? None extravagant, but at this hour of the night her mind conjured all kinds of fissures, gaping holes, ragged slits, cracks, his walls crazed like eggshell porcelain. Other than occasionally driving by at night, she hadn't visited his house in several months; she had no way to gauge its depreciation. In her mind's eye, and in the darkness, it sat as white as alabaster and pristine, *amid* life—situated at the pulsing heart of the most elaborately populated 50 square miles on earth—*housing* life, but unscarred by it.

Driving past, recently in daylight, however, she'd noticed a dangling gutter, two shutters hanging.

Maizie sighed against the screen, gazing out at the carport. A great placid moon hung in the sky, but that didn't help. It only brought tumbling forth, as in memory's landslide, the conversation she'd had with him a week before, when he'd unexpectedly popped in. She'd opened the door to find him there, his skin so milky, almost translucent. He was the only native Angelino she'd yet known who abhorred the sun; all blushes and colorations were transparent on him. And he did blush prettily after he'd stumbled in, flopped down on her sofa. "My friend is visiting," he told her.

She had cocked her head; the woman he dated was named Shannon. Other than her, Maizie wasn't certain who he might mean.

"You know," he said, "it's *that* time, the curse of Adam. My *monthlies.*"

She remembered laughing as he went on to explain that there was some evidence to suggest men experience monthly cycles, too, a condition characterized especially by a heaviness in the testicles. "Of course, a full moon just complicates things." He eyed her. "There's no doubt it influences large bodies of water. The thing is, it probably affects even a *glass* of water. I used to waiter," he said, "I remember how many trays of water I dumped on my way to customer tables. At certain times of the month the glasses almost seemed to *leap* from the trays. If a man's body is 96% water, just like a woman's why wouldn't the moon influence *him*, too?"

"Because you don't have moonstones," she said. She touched her lower abdomen. "I'm talking about ovaries."

He cupped his groin. "Yeah, but these feel like something John Glenn brought back on the Apollo. I'm having my period," he said. "I feel as if I crawled up out of the ocean last night, sprouted legs and arms, and joined the human race. Don't I look the least bit phosphorescent?"

They carried on in the same vein, and afterward she'd felt pleasantly invigorated; her own face in the hall mirror, when she walked him to the door, looked flushed. His nearness had launched her; she, like a statue, had been lifted high against the sky. The feeling couldn't sustain itself unsupported, though. It was a spun sugar castle sculpted atop a passing raincloud. A web of light built on air—to catch bricks. She crashed a few hours later, as off a drug. Hadn't seen him since.

Now, she turned from the window and in the grainy darkness made out her room. The sheets formed small peaks on her mattress, like stiff meringue, or crested surf. It was all known, it was what she had. Yes, one night he moved his hands over her body and moaned in her hair. She had said his name over and over, enjoying what was in her mouth.

Something murderous fanned its way, like a brushfire, through her torso. At least she *had* tasted it! Some people never would.

But, in life was that enough?

After standing in the kitchen and gulping down a cup of warmed milk, she tumbled into her bed as if into the wave that would carry her off, to the new world.

II

"They should have called it Ocean," she said. The group huddled around her, leaving a crescent-shaped space, from their toes to hers, of several feet in width, as if out of respect for something unveiled in all its mysteriousness before them. They looked where she pointed, made eye contact, all waiting in silence to be informed, for her to take them on the tour, acquaint them with the unknown; she passed her hands over the globe, drew their eyes up the wide expanse of blue, helped them see how entirely was the earth composed of water.

"Should have called it Ocean"—a little girl echoed the words; it was something Maizie said at least twice a day, sometimes more when the other tourguide was off and she took his groups around among the aquaria and other sea exhibits. It had a curious magical ring. Once, outside of work, when standing in the open fish market at Balboa Pier, mulling over the day's catch, considering the abalone, not the sea cucumbers, she'd said it. A beach bum—of the sort who sleep in the sand all day and haunt the U-Tote-M's by night—had stood next to her, talking with the fishermen and women. "You can live off the Pacific, man. Everything you need's right there. It's a big wet garden, you see? There's the fish, the shellfish. There's the seaweed."

Someone murmured disbelief.

"Yeah, *kelp* man. Eat the leaves like a salad, stuff the pods with rice, you know? 'S good," he said. "Wakame, nori, hij-ito, agar-agar, and so on, right?" And he looked at Maizie. That's when she delivered her Living World line.

He stared as if she'd pushed to the core of something incomprehensible. She was holding a whole snapper—head on; its tail lay wet against her wrist. No one spoke, or even moved, for several moments. It wasn't so much she who had created this silence, but a peculiar lassitude in the presence of a truth—something familiar to her from conducting tour groups. "Well, it's like a private smorgasboard. All you can eat." He had faced the sea and the setting sun, arms uplifted, as she'd seen people performing Tai Chi exercises do.

But it was all rote now, so petrifyingly second nature, guiding a group in among the cool stone chambers of Living World where were housed the ocean wonders, the walls always slick, the air always dank and smelling of a cellar— and dark, the tanks providing the only light, a pale, always shifting one. Advances in oceanography happened too grad-ually; Maizie rarely had new things to say. And the creatures were so well kept that few ever died. Besides, she knew them all, had seen everything the sea could offer and had been awed to silence a hundred stunning times over—but no longer. No new species would suddenly crop up; Nature wasn't hard at work designing something that would edify her. Not even a man riding a clam shell in over the breakers? A wet thing, half human, half amphibian, dragging its new legs up out of the surf? Maizie lead the group to a tank illuminated only with glowing red lights, began describing *lophius piscato-rius,* the angler fish: how it dwells in the ocean depths, fishes for its food, its fishing rod built-in, green and blue "head-lights" aglow as bait. Her own mind was submerged, not in the darkness of 500 feet but deep into precious woods, metals, stones, an interior fringed and beaded, scalloped and corded, drawn tight and scrolled at every corner—a magnificent structure erected high above sea level, topping a hill: so much gold and glass, satin and plush, so much tulipwood and red marble and malachite. She paced off the corridors of her lus-trous temple, as if measuring for area rugs, or furniture. She *had* helped Lee decorate the tabby house, *had* chosen the brindled, natural fabrics to match the exterior and soft fiber sculpture for the walls. "Can I *live* with this?" he'd asked, alone with her in a furniture warehouse, folding himself into a low-slung occasional chair, one she'd selected. They had walked from each well-appointed, if jam-packed, room to the next, their voices muted what with all the cork and baize, all the Herculon and Antron-nylon carpet. "Will I be happy with this chair? Could I read a novel, cover to cover, in this chair?" He hooked a leg over the arm when she smiled. "Shouldn't that always be the criteria when buying furniture? Imagine what you'll be doing in it, and then gauge your comfort?" To understand a week later that, during a solo outing, he'd chosen his own bedroom suit was to feel disappointment but not to be too terribly surprised. Besides, the longer she thought about it, the more likely it seemed, yes, she *had* helped him choose it—she'd been there. Hadn't they lain on 2 dozen mattresses, finding just the right one? And spread their hands over thousands of yards of sheets? Didn't they afterward drink Ethiopian Harrar and eat spice pogens, leaving the crumbs all over his new bed? She assuaged any further sadness by imagining that that day in the furniture warehouse something had come, at least for her, as their vision merged. He'd bought the chair and other pieces she suggested. "Would *you* for example, be comfortable with this?" he asked, slapping the fat cushions of a loveseat. "Could you *live* with it?" At the time she had scarcely thought about what that meant—in fact, it meant nothing unusual.

Since then it had.

Another trophy, polished as crystal, to decorate the mantle of her temple. Another trophy to take down, as now, to handle, to reflect back her face from its curved golden sides, and alight memory's long wick. But simultaneous to the warm glowing she felt inside, she knew it had been a year and a half: a year and a half in which she hadn't yet lived intimately enough, with him, to know if she could *live* with it or not. She had made Lee Greencastle the goal one strives a lifetime toward; usual, chronological time meant nothing when it came to him.

Now, Maizie finished guiding the tour, a tiny blue flame kindled within. And began the brief question and answer phase.

Were the Lionfish's quills poisonous?

Did Living World use paralyzing drugs when collecting the animals?

How far could an anemone walk in an hour?

Last month there had echoed forth a voice from far back in the chamber, where the dim aquarium tanks scattered no light, asking after the green flash which sometimes appears on the horizon as the sun sinks into the sea. Several people had stood aside, gazing back into the gloom. A family of eight parted down the center to let the man come forward, one little boy looking all around, seeming to shiver, as if in doubt the voice had come from anyone at all. The man had surfaced from the shadows, his limbs, his dimension, emerging from the dark. He walked forward, grinning.

Her heart had leapt out against her ribs, as if trying to escape. It was Lee.

The only other time he'd ever met her at work they'd gone for cocktails and poorman's lobster afterward. They'd shot three-par golf until midnight. They'd driven California 1 all the way to the San Buenaventura mission and back. After a moment, though, this time, Maizie's heart quieted. Her blood had seemed to slow. The man *looked* like Lee, in the dark; she caught her mistake. And tried to match Hane's smile. "You mean the Emerald Drop," she had said to him. She'd explained the rare atmospheric conditions necessary for the effect and then said, "In Spanish it is known as "la vida verde"—the green life. Some cultures of the Pacific and the Caribbean view it as an omen of good luck." She and Hanes went for dinner somewhere afterward, a dimly lit place in Trabuco Canyon.

Now the group, satisfied with her answers, began to break apart, to drift back toward other exhibits she'd taken them through, or to wander on outside to the beach, and Living World's open-air gift shop there—but not down to the water. The sea seemed bleached out, it faded in comparison to the aquarium riches inside. They were on display like the polished treasures in a jewelry case, its lid thrown back, soft baby spots trained on it. What roiled up in the waves came entangled in sea grass, was algae-covered, uncompromising, brown like the water, and unexplained. The world inside was pretty, maintained; out here it was raw.

Today the water looked like molten silver, and she squinted, sunlight melting into it. Pastel highlights shimmered on the surface, a peculiar sort of iridescence that stopped her in the sand and held her. Maizie had never seen such unusual colors afloat; it was like a lazy rainbow. Just when she thought she knew, thought she had water all figured, comfortably guiding her tours within the dark, wet chambers, she found she didn't understand at all. It kept its secrets—had its own life—and it was inaccessibly *private*. As if to dot all her i's, a porpoise popped up out of the water some 100 meters out, followed by two others, curving round, down, and up, as if attached to a huge, turning wheel. And then she saw him, along the moustache of high-tide, kicking at a length of kelp tangled around his ankle.

It was as if she'd never move again, as if she'd never draw another breath.

"Oh!" Lee said, shading his eyes to look up the beach, "At *last*," as though *she'd* kept him waiting.

It took less than a minute to move across the sand to him, and when she got there she stood, out of breath. When she didn't see him frequently she always on meeting Lee again had a renewed formidable sense of his charm. Alluring as that charm had ever been, it stood now like a monument in itself: robust, mighty, pulling her to it. All of him—his eyes, hair, the way the sun etched his lean silhouette—made her heart beat fast. "Nuclear holocaust scares me," she said, in an attempt at calm. "But not the way plastic does."

There was a pause in which he seemed to study her, then, "Plastic?" he said, as if encountering the word for the first time.

She pointed down to the multi-colored array caught in the tide line: bread bags, shot cases from the gun club at Lido beach, champagne corks. "Because it can't be destroyed," she told him. He gazed mildly off, seaward, and she, kicking off her sandals, bent to roll her pants legs. "I've always wondered about this," she said. She toed one of several tampon applicators within a 20 foot radius. "Do women come here in hoards to insert tampons? Does this have something to do with gravity's influence on the uterus?"

She waited for his laugh but it never came. He just stared out to the distant gray crease that was the horizon.

"Would this explain the mystery of PMS?" Maizie nudged him. "You're still having your period, right? You ought to know."

"What?" he said, turning. "Oh, *that*. It's sewage overflow," he said. "Whenever there's more rain than the sewer system can manage, raw sewage pours into the Pacific." His eyes were jumpy, meeting hers and not staying there for long but flitting out among the waves, out where several people in wetsuits waited, straddling their boards, for high surf.

"Yuck," she said after a bit.

Somewhere in the distance a gull screamed; a pelican wheeled 50 feet above the water then, collapsing like a wet rag dove down. It surfaced with some bit of silver twitching in its beak—but nothing else spectacular came leaping out of the water. Lee seemed as restless as the waves, giving his attention first to the horizon, then the foam breaking at his feet, and back again. He made an impatient clicking sound in his mouth, in counter-cadence to the sea. At a distance, the surfers bobbed up and down, waiting. They looked only part-human, their lower extremities board-shaped, arcuated, oblong, painted garish, high-gloss purples, reds, turquoise. They rose and fell on the sea swells, like stickpins fastened to an ever-buckling fabric.

"I'm so worried," he said. "I'm losing her, I know it." And Lee seized her hand so roughly two of her fingers twisted together. Within just a second he'd dropped her hand, but the throbbing remained. "I don't know what I'll do. I'm scared to death. Oh, Maizie," he moaned.

He didn't often call her by name; it, in his mouth, felt good. She savored that sensation, as if something sweet dissolved on her own tongue, before asking what was wrong. He told her, his voice a register higher than usual, how Shannon was undertaking an intensive job search in San Diego. "She'll just fall apart down there. You know how stressful it is, looking for work. What's she going to do for health insurance in between jobs? Besides, she's fragile," he said, "up here"—and he tapped the side of his head. "Shannon is a woman who needs someone to hold her together. Oh, goddammit. She needs *me.*"

Maizie had a difficult time imagining anyone falling apart in San Diego; it was so *under*whelming. "Why suddenly is she doing this?"

It was as if he couldn't look at her and say it. "To punish me."

Waves rushed in, hitting the beach with increasing frequency as the tide began to rise; tiny shells sparkled in the sand in its wake. The candlefish were running this time of year, and their golden bodies looked, rolling within the waves, as if suspended in great curved walls of green glass. "Lee, let's get a drink. Let's go over to the Crab Cooker. This place is depressing."

He hadn't seemed to hear her. "I'm mourning her already," he said, and he kept himself composed for several minutes. He said, "To lose...," and gazed off into the distance. Then, and she was not prepared for what followed, his face melted into a tormented mask of itself. He wept openly, staring out to sea.

She put her hand on his shoulder, then slid her arm around him—but a wave tussled forth; Lee stumbled just out of reach. Still, her voice was gentle. "Doesn't it seem unlikely she'd move 100 miles away just to punish you?"

He turned on her. "You don't know what she'd do. She's not stable. The things she'd do—! You can't imagine." Maizie looked past him. It was true. She knew little about Shannon—she liked knowing little about her. All the same it seemed he spoke less of her than himself. Shannon delicate? She was a sales rep. for a medical supply company. The woman had bark like a tree. He said, "You don't know what she did to my *house*."

"Huh?"

"Oh, skip it," he said.

She grabbed Lee by the arm so tightly she could feel his pulse. "Tell me."

His face was mottled red from crying; he wiped away the tears, and swallowed. "Painted it."

As a wave rushed over her feet, she felt an instant numbing, darts of ice up her ankles, and then the slight erosion, when the water carried some sand away, as if the land were sliding out from under her. Maizie nodded her head. She felt she'd have to dig with her heels all the way to China to steady herself against this blow. "Shannon painted it? In anger?"

"Look, I just don't like the color. *She* chose it. Didn't even ask me." He stared down at his feet. "We've argued about this for a week. It's the bedroom," he said. "I just don't feel at home." And then his gaze fixed her. "It's why I'm glad I can talk to you. I *do* feel at home with you."

A nova fired inside her. She saw herself skipping wildly across a great silver landscape, kicking up white dust around her—a tremendous freedom coursing through her body— stars aglow like hot jewels on a slab of onyx, their metalic light hanging high in the sky. Here, standing ankle-deep in the rising Pacific, though, Maizie was conscious only of rocking slightly forward on the balls of her feet.

"Give her up," she said.

He turned to her in pleading exasperation, as if she'd voiced the thing he, left to his own ingenuity, could not. "Oh—give her up!" He was shaking his head. "She's so fragile...," he said.

Just then shrieking laughter from among the surfers sliced the air; he jerked his head toward the west. On shore, waves were rushing in like white stallions; in the distance, swells gathered, came lumbering as slow as clouds forward. One swept the surfers, their boards, sea weed, fish, into it like a watery void that, as it gathered toward shore, arched ever upward, straining. It hung like a cliff for just a second in all its hugeness, then broke into a curl ten feet high. Bodies, boards were catapulted into the air; all surfaced several seconds later in the wave's calm after-sweep. One surfer on a green board managed to ride all the way to shore, and then tumbled into the foam near them. He stood up, giggling, his sleek, black wetsuit as thick as hide.

Someone somewhere applauded. Lee still studied the horizon. "Shannon's going to kill herself," he murmered.

Maizie had in the meantime turned to watch the man with the green board unzipping his suit, peeling it down as if molting. Underneath, he was a big blonde animal: golden hair on his chest, shoulders, pale curly hairs on his back that disappeared under the waistband of his Speedo. He shook the wetsuit and out flopped a small yellow fish; it twitched in the sand, as if breading itself in the gold dust, and then, the tide boiling in, disappeared into the sea. "Lee, what do you mean?" she said, turning back, a little impatient. "She's going to kill herself? By going to San Diego?"

"No," he said, "out there." She followed the length of his outstretched arm to the very tip of his pointing finger and then looked no farther. She knew what she'd find. Maizie breathed the air for a bit. When she asked how it was Shannon happened to choose *this* particular beach for surfing, the beach outside Living World, Lee said, *"I chose it. She's the one who wanted to surf. So I insisted. Because I knew I could talk to you. I knew we could talk."*

Sashes to mend. Crumbled stone to replace. Panes of quartz to polish. Windows to caulk. Silver to clean. Brass to burnish. Wainscot to dust. Floors to wax, and then all of it to do over again, starting in the left wing and working toward the right, back and forth for as long as it took. There was plenty to keep her occupied, to make a full, active life. Because talking—that was all she had with Lee.

He turned soft eyes on her. "I thought you'd help me feel better."

Tons of water rushed in, rushed out. It left things stranded on the sand, it carried things away. And capriciously— there seemed no pattern. "Do you?" she asked at last. "Feel better, I mean."

He stared uneasily toward the horizon, then turned back. He patted his belly as after a filling meal. "Yes. In fact I *do*."

"Then let her go." Maizie had positioned herself, without at first realizing, in such a way that he would, with a single sweeping glance, take them both in. She shifted her weight from one foot to the next but remained there before him.

Lee held out his hands, as if showing her how free they were. A smile split his lips. "I may let her go, but how could she ever let *me?*"

"Let you?"

"Go."

He did gaze past her now and kept his eyes steadily occupied there, with what he saw. When he spoke, his voice was a murmur. "It's as if she's part of my body. She's in me like a second heart. I am in thrall," he said. "My mouth is full of her. Full of her body. And it's not enough." He ran his tongue over his lips, as if the taste lingered there. "I can't *not* think of her."

At first Maizie only stared several incredulous moments, taking in all of him, how he stood letting her see his utter helplessness. Her own heart had set up an erratic cadence. "But do you imagine," she asked at last, "she thinks of *you?*"

Lee looked at her with the eyes that had just focussed, there in the distance, on Shannon, that had, the image inverted, presented Shannon to his brain to transform. *"Me,"* he said. He laughed heartily at that. "It's not necessary. Not even the point. Do you see?"

· The ocean roared; waves slammed the beach, sending tremors up through her heels. Somehow the words staggered out. "You help her," Maizie said.

He nodded once. "I help her." And with that he locked his fingers behind his head, elbows wide, stretching himself—satisfied—a man with his mission in life, and happy for it.

How had Maizie helped *him?* His eyes had turned faithfully seaward; they were clear now and, like the sea, the same pale, soothing shade. There seemed nothing more to do. And she stood several awkward moments beside him. Eventually, they said their goodbyes. As she made her way across the sand, a wrecking ball hung, in her mind's eye, from the end of its reinforced cable. It dangled in the sky like a volunteer planet. After several moments, though, it began to swing to and fro, as if some secret of gravity in the earth had stirred.

III

"He's gone," she insisted over the phone, "the man in my mind."

It was not a light that beckoned but, dimly, at the end of a dark, low-ceilinged corridor *Hanes* she saw; he was the way back to life: a man willing to hold her, kiss her, love her. She asked his forgiveness, when she called him; she asked for another chance. "He *is* gone," she told him. And two nights later, Hanes came for dinner. She served blackened redfish with dirty rice; he supplied a good Mondavi.

In the kitchen after dinner, as they were cleaning up and finishing the wine, Maizie kicked off her shoes. He'd asked about the small marine tank she kept on the counter, and she talked a little about it, about its carpet of lavender anemones, specimens she'd hand-collected while diving off Point Lobos with Lee. There had been no beach on the Point, only rock cliffs on which stood hundreds of brown pelicans; sea lions had rolled in the waves. Signs posted all along the coast had forbade the collection of plant material or sea creatures, but Maizie had never seen anemones of such an unusual shade— not even at Living World—and could not resist. While no one was looking, she'd eased a half dozen into a sealed pouch which Lee then stuffed down the front of his wetsuit, joking as they walked back to the car about the enormous bulge: "You don't suppose they stop every guy with a hard-on just because they think he might be stealing fish, d'you?" Standing, smiling before her aquarium, Maizie told Hanes none of this—but she felt it all. When she and Lee had returned to Orange County, *then* it had happened, *that* was the time, *her* moment: not that she got caught—that had never come about. But that they'd tumbled into his bed together, the first and only time. Now, she pointed out the school of tomato clownfish busily swimming about among the anemones. "They're the dogs of the sea," she said, tracing her finger in a wide figure eight on the glass. Several of the fish followed her movement, executing loops in the water. Hanes smiled at their tricks. "Can they fetch?" he said. It was all fun, his bending over the sink, hands hidden in the suds; her explaining the fish. Their Latin name was *tetradontiae,* she said— for the four razor-like teeth: two fused together on top, two on the bottom. She sprinkled dried brine shrimp onto the water's surface and asked him to turn off the faucet. "So we can listen to them eat." They bowed their heads near the tank, waiting, and were rewarded with a faint gnawing sound, a tiny noise, like gentle filing. Both erupted into laughter at the same moment. They were near enough to kiss, to stare deeply into each other's eyes, to—he shifted just slightly—feel their thighs rub. Stillness hung thick; only a bubble spray from the aquarium's airstone hummed in the silence. Hanes leaned closer and their lips touched; his mouth was richly flavored, tasting of the dinner, the wine. His hand slipped behind to arch her body upward against him, then gracefully beneath the folds of her blouse to explore her bare back. She felt her body open, the sensation he stirred wash through her. When he raised her blouse, she yielded to the light pressure of his fingers and then his lips grazing her nipples. She shuddered. Even her breathing in the stillness seemed loud.

But not as loud as the phone ringing in the next instant; it shrieked. They both jerked, scaring the tomato clowns who zigzagged crazily about the aquarium, losing their color.

Maizie's phone was white; it hung at hip-level from the butcher block island, as if holstered there. She stared at it, at first not budging. It was *that* delicate, their moment.

When she did at last answer the phone, Lee's voice came crackling over the line.

And Maizie excused herself, took the call in the bedroom, coming back out after she'd picked up the receiver so she could hang the other up. Hanes had put his hands back down in the dishwater; he turned profile as she lied to him, saying it was some silly family matter, that it would only take a minute.

She lay across her bed. "Don't say no," Lee said.

Maizie laughed abruptly. "That's a dangerous demand." What she heard over the line, though, told her that that was the wrong tone to take; he sobbed once, then sighed.

"Oh, help me. It's falling to pieces. It's collapsing around me."

"The house?"

She heard him blow his nose. "Well, a valance crashed to the floor. And, yeah, I can't fix it now." He seemed to struggle with himself; she heard a low, bitter murmur, then: "I'm too—*drunk*"—the word itself a sob.

For a moment she feared he'd hang up. "The valance? In which room? The den? Or in the living room?"

He paused. The line hummed with static. From the kitchen Hanes cleared his throat. "Oh, what's it matter?" Lee threw in. "Just tell me, will you help?"and then, "She's gone. She's left me." As if Maizie's silence signalled a lack of comprehension, he explained. "Shannon," he whispered. "Shannon, Shannon, Shannon." The word slurred into a chant.

Maizies's hands felt heavy as she hung up the receiver.

Back in the kitchen, she leaned against the butcher block, thinking in the next instant she'd throw herself down on it as sacrifice. Hanes stared abstractedly at the aquarium, then gave her a pinched, ironic smile. "That was your brother, right?"

She looked at him a little. Her own voice, when it came,

was low. "It's my life."

He flung the dish towel into the dining alcove. "Bullshit. You don't live anywhere. I mean, has someone hugged you lately? Have you been kissed? Before tonight, I'm saying. Has anyone made love to you and then held you afterward? Caressed you? Touched you in any particular way? Slept with you all night? No?" With each question he paced about, bumping the counter, knocking an elbow against the refrigerator, stumbling over a doorstop. At last he stood before her; his breath felt hot on her face. "Where *do* you live, Maizie? And when? When I'm not around? Only up here?" he said pushing his palm against her forehead so her head snapped back.

She clamped her fingers around his hand and forced it down against the butcher block. The words, when uttered, came like a growl from deep within her; she felt them jet up from the soles of her feet, surge from the beds of her toenails. "Leave me."

They stood faced off like animals ready to begin ripping at each other. Then he was shaking his head, backing away from her, out of the kitchen, slipping through her door, receding like tide, as though pulled back to his habitat—the palpable world, the well-founded, sturdy one—heeding irresistibly its call.

IV

She heard it, habitat's siren lure.

Something native to her own blood urged her forward, tugged her, as with the unreasoning power of gravity. She could stand fast, endure it, for a time—but would inevitably yield. It was sweet, surrendering to her calling; she always let it pull her through the maze-like streets of Cathedral City to stand in the tabby house's pale radiance, at Lee Greencastle's door.

But it was different, his threshold, this time.

No lights shone from any window—no candles were aglow this time—and although they hadn't spoken since the night she'd hung up on him, she knew he'd be there. It was *his* habitat, his element, at least in her mind. He was in it as she was in it: thick. He was in it like an oyster in its shell.

Lee hadn't for several minutes answered the door upon

her knocking, and she'd stood in the odd pearlescent light which reflected off the sides of the house, waiting. There *it* thrived, her other life. Hadn't she bathed with Lee in a tub of gold-veined marble, bubbles clinging like ocean froth to their skin? And eaten hot cinnamon rolls while swinging in a silk hammock, icing melting between their fingers? No. And she hadn't gone to Disneyland with him either, paying the exorbitant admission fee not for the rides and amusements but for the sweets and chicory brew in the "French Quarter." They had not split a half dozen beignets and sat—powdered sugar dusting their lips and fingers—dangling their feet in the moat around Snow White's castle. Eyes toward Tomorrowland. At the same time she watched it happen, she knew it hadn't. When thinking clearly, when knowing herself anchored to life, and not just tethered at the ankles or moored to it—but *entwined,* all her dangling ends woven up into the real world, herself dressed deeply in the warmth of living, Maizie saw it all. Her memories then seemed—well, what they were. The temple appeared as fixed as a death mask, hollow like catacombs; it had the deserted air of a place that houses no life. She couldn't hear footsteps echoing down any hallways. No one would ever breathe there again, no window ever be cracked open. Night-robbers, poachers and thieves, carried parts of the temple away: ornate door jambs, rolled Persian rugs, mantle pieces of carved rosewood; ghouls swiped, filched, stole, made off with what was inside, took what belonged to no one, cleaning it, the way vultures clean up after a death.

Maizie saw.

They'd had so little chance to love—! And then for the time they had been together it wasn't love so much as it was a frantic tumble, and shyness afterward. Their sleeping together was a mistake, something she'd lived long enough to see taken back, ripped from her—by *living past the morning after.* It now seemed some error of fate which, without explanation or apology, fate had erased.

While waiting for Lee to answer the door, she had rubbed her hand idly along the doorjamb. That chalky substance had sunk into her fingerprints, into the wrinkles and crevices of her palm.

Now, standing beside a packing crate in his living room, Maizie looked at that faint white dusting. What was it they said about the lifeline, and which hand, left or right, did they mean? A steady, unbroken line meant long, calm life? What of the one splintered, like hers, in the middle? After the first life, was there another? Could she rob her own grave and begin anew? Studying it, she stood very still, her pounding heart the only movement.

He hadn't turned any lights on; he couldn't: Cal-Edison had disconnected service. He'd said, "You're wondering why we're sitting in the dark? It's not that I don't have the money. It's just that I don't care." All the take-out containers strewn about—Pioneer Chicken, Carl's Jr., Me 'n Ed's Pizza—underscored his remark. The place smelled sweetly of rot.

Light flickered through the drapes, as cars passed outside, and seeped like some smoky liquid across the floor. Shadows hung about the corners of the room, as if ready to drag the house down, all Lee's unhappiness hanging like lead.

Or *hers*.

Because he'd made his decision, he'd made up his mind. He, technically speaking, was free. Before she'd so much as taken her seat, he'd told her. "I listed the house with Coldwell Banker."

Maizie didn't immediately sit but remained leaning against the living room arch, staring back into the dark for some time. When she turned, it was with so sinking a heart, a sensation so deeply disquieting, that as he lifted his head to meet her gaze he instantly cast his eyes to the floor. "Don't look at me like that. It's falling apart. You can't see the water spots on the ceiling, but they're there. The gutters are shot. The plumbing, too. My ice plants are dying. Have you noticed the lawn is dead? Oh, Christ."

"You mean *you* were," she said after scrutinizing him a little in the dimness. "Dying."

He nodded solemn assent. "I was dying. I had life with her here. And I want it back. So I've got to go." Their eyes met, and he, absurdly, brightened. "In San Diego, I know I can find work with more pay. The air's cleaner. I won't have to hassle with freeways. I can drive the surface streets there. It's not even looked upon as an eccentricity! There's Balboa Park. And the zoo and, look "—he held both hands out—" Sea World, if you please. The desert's closer. So are the mountains. And Mexico. My realtor said I could expect a hundred thou-fifty for all this. And since you know things are so much cheaper down there . . . " He leaned comfortably back, caught up in his own imagining.

Breathe clean air. Strike it rich. Throw peanuts to the elephants. Live in the town of the magically paved, golden surface streets. It was all out of a storybook: the prince who finds a castle for under a hundred thou-fifty and lives there with the beautiful princess. His child-like simplicity stunned her; she gaped at him, not invidiously or cynically, but in awe.

Because the worst had nothing to do with his naivete.

He was in love.

Maizie stared at that fact as at a deformity, some hated joke of Nature never to be undone. It flaunted itself naked before her, and she watched it pass.

"I thought of all the life I'd had with her," Lee was saying. "I can't give it up. All that she and I have done! The significant moments we've shared. And the beauty. The woman has such an appreciation. Camping at Big Bear. Rappelling Mt. Baldy. Diving off Point Lobos. Shooting rockets at Joshua Tree. I can't give it up. Not any bit of it! To give up would be to erase my own *history*. How would I know who I am?"

There was a silence and then, "Point Lobos?" she said.

He threw his hands out before him as if to protest. "None of it. I refuse. I can't sacrifice any of it."

"You two never went diving at Point Lobos," she said.

He blinked. "Yes. In '82."

She cocked her head. "In '82 Point Lobos was quarantined, from hazardous waste. I remember because *I* wanted to go diving then. Didn't get around to it until the next season. You remember," she said.

He frowned. "She was with me. We speared albacore. She collected anemones from the tidepools."

"You *think* you two went."

"What do you mean? You know damn well I went diving at Point Lobos. How do you think I got this?" And he flexed his ring finger before her, showing her the ugly red scar from where the tip had nearly been severed and now rejoined: the bite of a baby Great White.

She stared as if she'd been struck between the eyes with a stone. "You want so badly to have had a life with her that now you're dreaming one up! You and she didn't go diving at Point Lobos." Nothing—not even the air—stirred. They faced each other in the quiet, sweet-smelling rot, the darkness as heavy as standing water. It seemed neither of them would ever move again. Then the words tumbled out. *"We* did. Are you going to tell me you don't at all remember?" Looking at him, her eyes filled.

It was as if he'd frozen where he sat; he shrugged and held that pose several moments. She could almost hear him pillaging memory's recesses, flinging doors open, throwing lids off boxes, dumping drawers, all the contents scattering about. Even in the dark she could see the look of amazement flush slowly across his features, and then recognition. His shoulders relaxed. "Christ, you're right. How could I forget?" He looked at his finger.

That gesture seemed so singularly stupid.

Flames leapt before her eyes. So he had done as she had: lived his life over in the way he'd wanted it. He had himself a little temple somewhere, too, had erected marble walls, bought iron vases inlaid with gold, designed a barrel-vaulted ceiling of white ornamental plaster that was as pure as frosting on a wedding cake—and just as elaborate.

Or maybe his temple was made of straw.

Lee Greencastle might be anything. *She* built *him* up. He probably didn't even like cinnamon rolls or beignets, this mysterious creature who sat across from her, all his motives and contingencies, his odd, beautiful dreams of happiness, bundled inaccessibly within. What did she truly know, except what she invented for her own cache of suffering? All the smiles, the caresses, the leading words, and the moments of comfort were, on Lee's part, inexpensive gifts, but unadorned all the same. Cheap. The things of love had languished around her as she'd waited for him. There had been Hanes, a man perfectly willing to love, and she'd abstained. In an extravagantly shabby way. Silly to think you could have a religion without martyrdom or without celibacy to an idea. And the virgin sacrifice. Because walled up in her memories, she'd held her breath, certain *Lee* kept all the treasures carefully hoarded under *his* hands.

Now, the shining marble walls shimmered, as through heat; flames leapt from every opening, licked the hard, white sides. When she looked again, she saw a high pyramid of ash, the wind gradually razing it. Her temple had less existence than, say, smoke.

"Jesus," he was saying, "I hate to pack. Taking it all apart here"—he shifted both hands far to the right and then, in an instant, far to the left—"putting it back together there." He shook his head when their eyes met.

He was a guy.

And this was just someone's house, with its myriad cooking smells, its dust bunnies, its dinner dishes piled in the sink, the closet doors closed on its mysteries. Any kind of life might be available in it: heart pounding, blood coursing, the body maintaining its warmth of 98.6

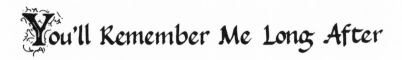

You'll Remember Me Long After

"**Y**ou've bought Andy some expensive gifts. That, for instance," Mrs. Guiginti said; she stood in the drive next to her Cadillac. Louise followed her gaze to a candy-apple red motorcycle parked under the carport, sunlight like half-moons shining on its glossy surface. "I guess it costs a little more, trying to keep him."

A pale cloud of smog drifted past the mountain range directly behind Louise's house, then scooted off across the desert like a pink curtain, but she felt no breeze. It was only 7 a.m. and her blouse already stuck to her back. "That bike was a gift," she told her, "not an obligation."

Mrs. Guiginti smiled at that and said, "I *know* it's an old tune, but his father and I would like to see him come back home." Her eyes were pale and watery and red-rimmed—but naturally so, Louise thought, not brought about by any excess of emotion here—and also somewhat shaded by the wide bill of her straw golfing hat. She smelled pleasantly of lavender, but her upper lip looked damp with perspiration. "Then there's the matter of his going on to finish school," Mrs. Guiginti said. She toyed with the brass clasp of her canvas clutch bag, snapping it, clicking it, rubbing the beaded tips. "This may sound hard to you now, but we do still control the purse strings for Andy. And we can cut him off, just like that, too," she said. "If it comes to that. Or did you think we wouldn't try something like that?"

"I don't think about what you people might do." Louise took a step nearer the drive, bristles of grass poking in the sides of her sandals. She said, as if enumerating, "Andy has made his decision, it is his life. Seems to me there is little you can do about it, he *is* of legal age . . ."

"So smart," Mrs. Guiginti said, her frown becoming even more pronounced so that the corners of her mouth dropped a bit. She gestured at Louise. "Look at you," she said. "Your hair. You're ridiculous."

Louise glanced sideways and found herself in the black tinted glass of the windshield; she and Andy had both gotten fluffy punk-style haircuts, just as jokes, as something new to do. Now, when they were together, she could feel their sameness: two identical spiked heads, except that Andy's hairline was wild with cowlicks. Her scalp still felt numb and still prickly when she passed her hand back and forth through her hair. She glimpsed her reflection there in the tinted glass— the hair still new enough to shock.

"Aren't you getting a little long in the tooth for that?" Mrs. Guiginti said. She glowered from beneath the golden visor; for several moments her eyes did not waver at all. "Listen to me, dolly, his youth is going to burn a hole in your pocket. It's going to bankrupt you where you stand."

"LEAVE," Louise thundered; she flung her arm out to point the way.

Mrs. Guiginti stood her ground but her hand trembled as she passed it over the hood of the Cadillac; she smoothed with her hand, as if preoccupied with a flaw in the paint, and she stroked, watching her fingers. Then, slapping the canvas clutch bag flat to her chest, and squaring her shoulders, she tried to dash past Louise.

With a dodge to the right, Louise stopped her and gripped her around the bicep. Mrs. Guiginti jerked her fist back, business-like, but Louise squeezed the woman close in a boxer's clutch, and began a scuffle that reminded her of slow-dancing. Eventually she walked her backwards five paces and then shoved her against the Cadillac. Mrs. Guiginti grunted softly and slumped on the fender. Louise said, "You're going to have a stroke. Tangling with me in this heat."

"Okay. Enough," Mrs. Guiginti breathed. She shook her arm loose and they stood, panting slightly. The golf visor had gone cock-eyed.

After Mrs. Guiginti started her car and put her sunglasses on, she rolled down the window of the Cadillac in one smooth sheet. "Can you pay for his tuition?" she said over the low engine noise. "What about his Palo Alto rent?"

Louise lunged forward, as if to leap through the glass. "Rawr!" she said.

Mrs. Guiginti's lips parted with a dry soft pop.

The smooth pane of black shot back up.

****

Louise developed assembly-language programs for Satellite Software; after six years the company had transferred her from Orange County to the desert, a less desirable location but a stint expected of most employees, on the climb up. They had moved her in the summer on the 16th consecutive day of the eventual 2 month long 120 degree spell Thousand Palms had suffered. No one went outside between 10 a.m. and 6 p.m. All stores opened early, closed, and then reopened to do business late; nights cooled to 95. The nearest electrical power source stood an entire mountain range away in the Los Angeles basin, making air conditioning an impractical expense. Most people used Desert Coolers, instead: enormous fans housed in squat shelters that crouched atop rooves and which could pull a steady breeze throughout the rooms. She estimated the wind her Desert Cooler generated sometimes gusted to 5 miles per hour—on low cycle. (Once, on high, the sports section of the *L.A. Times* had leapt up off the kitchen table to dance.) But it gave necessary relief. In August, Louise emerged from a carwash and turned her windshield wipers on to find the rubber had dried and shriveled in the heat, unable now even to squeegee a few drops of water away. The house she'd bought had an inground pool, but by September the thought of doing laps in hot water wore her out. So she joined Rancho Mirage, a health club, and began going early—taking a tennis class from the pro—to get a sense of community: people outside doing things.

"*Tennis,*" she'd grumbled her first day at Rancho Mirage—"at four in the morning, for Christ's sake!" Sunrise spread an indigo band just behind the Chocolate Mountains, and a blonde young man who stood courtside folding a pile of snowy white towels had laughed. His smile revealed dazzling teeth, and Louise experienced the first friendly feeling she'd had since moving to Thousand Palms.

An hour later when she, still unused to the pervading heat, dropped her racket and steadied herself against the chain link fence, a prickly sensation spreading across her scalp like some chilling rash, the blonde young man had appeared with a damp towel and a tumbler of ice water. She'd draped the towel over her head and drunk the water immediately, despite his admonishment to sip slowly, and then, crouched down, let him massage her temples with the ice. "Thousand Palms," she'd muttered cynically. "anyone ever count them?"

The feel of his fingers lulled her. "Thousand and one," he'd said.

She grinned. "You mean this is the desert's version of a baker's dozen?"

Droplets rolled down the sides of her face.

" 'Rock and no water and the sandy road'," he quoted.

She stared up into eyes that were the green of chipped bottle glass. *He* was a mirage.

They went to dinner a couple nights later and began keeping company together; he worked 10 hours a week at the club while accumulating credits at College del Sol, his major still undeclared. Andy had lived on the desert all his life; he had watched greenhorns, the snowbirds, come and go. That winter, after moving in, he said he could help Louise go native:

She learned the trick of stashing her windshield wipers in the trunk.

And keeping Saran wrap in the glovebox: if she broke

down in some remote area she could dig a hole, place a layer of wrap over it, and drink the condensation it made, like water.

Two refrigerators crowded her kitchen now—one just for making ice and storing cold drinks.

It took three vigorous sets of tennis to tire her any longer.

****

All the water had been drained from the pool 2 weeks ago and Andy was in the deep end now, hanging on a ladder, singing. A stained cloth tarp was spread below him. He held on with his elbow and stirred paint in a Folger's can with a brush. Louise circled the deck so that she stood above him, her tall shadow draped in the evening sun across the diving board. His voice banged off the sides of the empty pool and seemed to ring as it reached her.

"You send cold chills up and down my spi-ine,

We kiss for thrills but you draw the line—oh, baby.

Cause your mama told you that love ain't ri-ight... "

She knelt and made as if to shake the ladder.

"Hey," he said. He spattered flecks of emerald green near the tip of the pool wall and bent close, holding his wrist steady. The curved outline of a sea serpent rose under his brush.

Louise leaned over the edge so she could see all four walls at once. "Fabulous stuff," she said. An entire universe of cartoon characters was taking shape—mural fashion—in her pool. He called it Mukfa, some mythical world that consisted of an island, the ocean that surrounded it, and all the inhabitants of both: angler fish, purple turtles, shimmering sea shells, one exceedingly wiry, tweed-suited gentleman who was an air traffic controller for William Henry Esterplo International—the only Mukfa airport that offered transoceanic flights, Andy had once informed her. She'd looked at him, then away, and quickly back, the exaggerated doubletake. "You lie next to me, dreaming all this stuff?" she'd asked. A few days later Andy had told her he'd ground a special pigment so that all the mermaids of Mukfa could have eyes like hers—a bluish jade green color, and large.

Louise had gazed at where he'd painted them, the lovely bodies languishing on peachy coral reefs. "Why, the resemblance is uncanny," she'd said. "The eyes, the hair, the three breasts."

He laughed and looked at the mermaids, their tri-nipples tipped with sparkly pink. "Well, one to grow on," he told her.

Now, the ladder thumped against the side of the pool as

he climbed up, his toes nearly prehensile on the rungs; he balanced there at the top. His blonde hair was dark with sweat and speckled in places with exotic mixes of blues, pinks, yellows. It even sparkled. "Fabulous," she murmured, turning to him.

A blush colored either cheek as he smiled. One tiny spot of green glistened on his slightly moist lower lip.

"I know she was here today. There are new skidmarks on the drive," he said. "What'd you do—throw yourself in front of Ma's hog to keep her off the property?"

Memory of the morning twisted up inside Louise. "Oh, goddamn. To hear her talk—! She makes it sound like I'm on the short side of the *market*. Like your youth and my age constitute some highly speculative risk I've taken."

Andy wiped his hands on a paint rag. "Hah!"

A vein seemed to tie itself into a square knot at her temple. Louise spoke, inhaling sharply, as if surprised in advance at what she'd say. "And she said your father said you can forget about Stanford in the fall."

It was as though his knees might buckle beneath him. He wadded the paint rag and hurled it across the deck. "Oh, Lordy, Stanford!" he cried. "They act like their money's the only road to Stanford." He snatched up the rag and put it with the rest of his paint tools. "Can you believe I come from those people?"

She was shaking her head. "Look, it's your decision, and we've talked about that all along. Don't let *them* make up your mind. Now, you've mentioned the possibility of staying on down here. Of finishing up at College del Sol. Okay, I mean, it's up to you."

"Sure," he said. He stared out across the deck, and Louise followed his gaze into the distance, out past the mountain range behind her house that was soft-looking, like heavy fabric bunched up on the horizon, and colored a deep, velvety purple, and found herself peering into the wide blue-nothing of sky, a vista interrupted only by that thin line where mountains and sky joined which seemed to burn green at dawn but now appeared orange in the waning sun. Louise saw swirls and skating patterns in the liquid on the surface of her eyes, but nothing else moved. "*You* have to decide where home is," she said.

Beside her, Andy twitched, as if waking, and she focused her attention back on him, the yard, her house, real things. He said, "And I've got time to think of all that."

Though she had not reached out for him, he moved just

beyond the space in which she could have comfortably done so. He studied his handiwork—Mukfa. "Oh, yeah," he said, "A Vic Michaels called. From the Corona del Yermo Anti-Nuclear Alliance." He got down on his knees and began scraping with his thumbnail at some green paint that had trickled down the side of the pool; then he looked up, curiously. "Does this guy know something about me?"

Louise shrugged. She'd met him at a rally, before Andy, a gregarious, blunt man. "I've never mentioned you to him. In fact, I haven't seen him since winter. He got married, or something."

"Because when I told him I was taking your phone messages, the guy"—Andy paused just a beat—"chuckled."

"Well," Louise said—but word of the Alliance had reminded her, and she was preoccupied, searching for a newspaper clipping in her handbag. "They found radioactive sand on the beach at Balboa that has the identical nuclear magnetic resonance to contaminated sand found last week near Corona del Yermo. Did you know that weird cholla cactuses are growing outside the power plant? The needles are coming in hot! *How* did this happen? *No one* seems to know." She handed him a single-column article entitled "Corona del Yermo Safety Suspect."

He skimmed it; the text described how the radioactive agent, californium, produced only at the power plant on the high desert, was found at Balboa pier. Authorities theorized recent Santa Ana winds would have carried the alleged waste to the coast. "You should go fight," he told her, and handed the clipping back.

She exhaled roughly. "It's pervasive! How do you fight bureaucrats?" she stammered. "That sand's probably all washed out to sea by now."

"Or been shipped down to Mexico, to make Fiestaware."

Louise held her hand up between them, showing him the flat of her palm, fingers splayed. "Don't kid about this one, Andy. I care too much about what goes on on that coast. I *come* from there," she told him. "I know it isn't precious to you. No, all you've known is the dry, the bleached out, the arid."

His ribs expanded as he breathed; in the stillness, the thrash of a freeway 5 miles distant reached her. She glanced irritatedly about and then her gaze settled on Mukfa. "I mean, that paint, Andy—that glittery stuff? Is it metal flake? Mica?" She swallowed. "Radium paint?"

He had stopped scraping the spot of green and now

squinted up at her as if into the sun. "I *told* you. I'm not going to pollute your pool. Or endanger your cells." He grinned. "Your children won't be running around the desert with cabbage heads."

"In the *County*," she heard herself say, "not the desert. I'll be back in Orange County by then."

Andy nodded his head once and then, blinking, stared off into a space exactly perpendicular to her. She turned to see what he saw: sunlight cutting shadows on the violet mountains; fair, frail squalls of pink sweeping down the pass behind them.

"Baby boom," he whispered.

She whirled. "What?"

He knelt and scraped sullenly at the green. "You heard me."

Sweat evaporated just as soon as it formed on her skin, and despite the heat, she shuddered.

It was their sore spot.

A month back they had both been sitting in the living room, over an open NEWSWEEK, studying the photo of an artificial heart that had been implanted in a man's chest. "It'll pump the fountain of youth," Louise had said. The article described all the features of the device, as if it were a V-8 engine; the man had suffered several strokes since implantation.

Andy said, "The people of your generation are in love with immortality."

She perked up, as if she'd been prodded. "Well, I think any generation loves immortality."

"Don't get me wrong," he said. "I love long life. But I'm saying they're pouring a lot of research into this one particular area. And *it's only a tiny part* of cardiac technology. What about congenital heart murmurs? And atherosclerosis? Rheumatic fever," he said. "What about mitral stenosis? I'm saying your generation has begun to worry about dying, and because there are more of you, we *all* have to worry about it. It's everywhere: TV, in news magazines," he said, and he jabbed the pages in front of them—"at nuclear rallies, for God's sake!"

"You mean like the one we went to at Corona del Yermo?"

He shrugged. "The threat of nuclear devastation is your Boogie Man. Maybe it's a symptom of the mid-life crisis. Who knows?" He leaned back against the sofa and laughed. "You people," he said. "If I were smart, I'd know what field to go into—Mortuary Science! There was a Baby Boom, and there will surely be a Death Boom, too."

"So you're going to be there to clean up."

"Perhaps literally," he cried. "I mean, College del Sol *does* have a certificate program in Mortuary Science. And," he said, glancing away, "If I'm not mistaken Stanford does, too. When you people drop dead, I could come into a cornucopia of opportunity such as you can scarcely imagine."

Silent moments passed.

And then Louise did the thing she swore she never would. "Well, you're young." She smiled. "But let me tell you, you'll never be so young as on the day you die."

Andy clutched at his solar plexus, as if he'd been stabbed. "Oh, my *dear*," he said. "What the hell's that mean?"

Louise leaned toward him. "No one's ready to go. Ever. Not under any circumstances," she said. "Most people *do* think a painful, huffing, puffing, mechanical pump of a heart spazzing away in their chests would be better than death. Just *ask*."

"You are born," he had told her, thrusting first his left arm out from his side, his hand open and curved, as if holding something. "And you will die," he'd said, doing the same with his right arm. Looking on, her pulse throbbed at the base of her jaw. It felt as though they were posing for a photograph. Then she collapsed into merriment. Because, holding that absurd position, he looked like Justice—except he wore no blindfold.

That had been last month, a Friday evening, around the time Mrs. Guiginti had been harassing them through the mail, sending sardonic messages and cards—for instance on Mother's Day—just before Louise had contacted the authorities.

Now, she studied the clipping in her hand, her eyes skipping from word to word: high desert, hazard, californium. "Never in Orange County," she was saying. "No one would be that lax. That *inane*," she said. "It just wouldn't happen."

Andy rose from the side of the pool and clamped his hand completely around her wrist. "I'm not the desert. I just come from there."

His skin was warm, and his gaze enveloped her where she stood, as if the gazing, chipped green of his eyes could touch her. The thing she couldn't say welled up in her. *And now you're going to leave.*

****

Louise guided her cart down the produce aisle at the supermarket and there, like the fulfillment of some prophesy, stood Vic Michaels at one of the electronic game machines at the front of the store. Louise stopped in mid-aisle and stood open-mouthed, as if observing silence before a monument. A shopper cleared her throat behind her and Louise moved aside to let the woman pass. Vic had his face pressed up against the machine's viewfinder and he twisted lever controls in his hands. He put his body into it, drawing the shoulders up, bending at the knees, and swinging his hips at just the right moment, doing some kind of exotic dance, belly-up, to the machine. Luminous tanks and flying saucers crossed the screen before him, giving his face and neck a weird phosphor glow.

Louise pushed toward him, her cart loose-wheeled and hopping up on the fake-brick flooring. She stopped at his elbow. He wore a braided cowboy-length bola that was laced through his collar like a necktie and had a large cabochon slide of red turquoise; its pointed silver tips clicked against the plexiglass as he leaned into the machine, as he twisted back and forth. "That one cheats," she said.

He glanced away, squinty-eyed. "Well, God Almighty!" he said. Then he frowned and passed his hand pancake fashion over the top of his head. "Honey, your hair," he said, a little too loudly. "How awful!"

She saw from the corner of her eye a bag boy whispering to a young cashier, the brown paper bag in his hands twitching as he giggled.

When Vic turned back, an enemy tank fired a stem of yellow light, and the screen cracked before him, then froze, all the tanks fixed in attitudes of ceasefire. He made a mock kick at the machine and grinned at her. "I can't keep my hands off the son of a bitch," he told her. "Every time I see one I *have* to play. I'm like a cat unable to resist dangling string." He stuck his finger in the coin return and then walked with her, stopping near the check-out stand as she examined a display of condiments. He sighed, as if the sight of all those bottles made him weary. "Yeah, we've got to fight the good fight now," he said. "I'm sure you heard about the Newport Beach disaster..." Vic leaned in conspiratorially, as if what he referred to had not been publicly reported.

"Well, you mean at Balboa," she said.

He threw his square, thick-fingered hands up before him. "Newport Beach, Balboa, they're so close it confuses me. Where does one end and the other begin? Most people can't tell you. The important thing is, *it* happened. Now the Alliance has to scheme about that, decide what to do, and stuff." His voice trailed off as he watched her choose Heinz 57 over A-1. "Hey, you haven't asked me how marital bliss is yet."

She raised her eyebrows. "Well?"

He yanked his bola up, like a noose, and groaned, as if in pain. "It's over. Everything but the legalities. I slept last night in the Scirroco."

"I'm sad for you," she said.

"Yeah," he said. Vic rolled his eyes and looked at her from the side. "*Now* you ask. *Now* you want to know. *You* could've found out first hand, if you'd stuck by me. Right? Oh, but you go and get yourself a fancy answering service, yes indeed."

She studied his bland, round face for several moments. "I don't go for that talk, Vic. Andy lives with me."

He nodded enthusiastically. "Well, okay, I'd been hearing about you and Doc Guiginti's kid. Folks at the Alliance are buzzing about it."

"Oh, bullshit, Vic."

"Honey, who are you kidding?" he said. "they all know old man Guiginti. But, listen, when I first heard, I thought they were linking you with *him*. Swear to God," Vic said. His laughter sounded like bawling. "He's my chiropractor," he said. "The guy weighs 250 at least. I said, no, that's not Louise."

As they turned the corner a woman thrust a foil-wrapped platter loaded with steaming sausages before them, blocking their way. She had powerful-looking forearms and an apron tied high under her armpits. The woman held the platter with one hand and with the other fried the meat in an electric skillet, rags of steam drifting up around her hands as she worked the sausage, as she turned it with a fork and moved it around. The obstructing platter seemed less an invitation than a command, and they each selected a sausage from it.

"So, you and Junior," Vic said, after Louise had eaten her sausage and stood holding the toothpick. He touched her hair lightly and she could tell from his eyes that he wasn't quite sure what it would feel like when he did. "When you don't talk about your age difference, what do you talk about? Your hair?"

Louise heard herself answer perhaps too quickly. "Everything! Right now he's doing my pool. Paints. Lots of stencils. Fiberglass coatings that shimmer in the dark." She didn't care for the way Vic was staring at her. She said, "You'll have to stop by and see it."

"Your pool!" Vic laughed. "*I* would've painted your pool. Yeah, your pool." He said, "Oh, Christ, Louise, it's wasted on youth, tell me that. Tell me the young are unappreciative. I'm a paunchy divorced man. I need my illusions." He ate the sausage and slid the toothpick quickly behind a pyramid of canned goods.

Her cart banged into a display of canned peas. "Why make this so mysterious? Andy's not from Pluto."

"Because yours is an enviable position, Louise. Back at the Allaince no one's quite sure about what this means or where it will lead," he said, "but we're all a little green about it. Maybe you'll start a trend." He stopped. "Does it cheat death, Louise? Is it the juice of resurrection, like the fellow says?"

"Is *what?*"

"In fact, I drive home by way of the high school these days. The more illicit, you know. I deserve to be born again, too," and his bellow rang out among the food.

"Illicit!" she said and felt her lips stick to her teeth. "He watches TV and studies, and I fiddle with my IBM. Is that illicit? You make it sound like a lot more fun than I'm having."

Vic chuckled. "Well, Louise, let me tell you. Someone great once said something to the effect that having your youth twice is like having a second wind. Why, it's like opening night after a dress rehearsal." He smiled. "It's also a miracle, Louise. And miracles are expensive. If you want them to pay, you have to borrow."

"Vic, you've been listening to the wrong people. Come home with me. See with the naked eye how normal it all is. The pool," she told him. "It's good."

He threw back his head. "The *pool*, she says." He looked down at her cart and Louise watched as he surveyed the items there, as he regarded the scented candles, the two gourmet-cut steaks, the bottle of wine, the ginseng body rub, the box of bubble bath. He looked up at her.

"Green, Louise," he said. "Absolutely green."

He fastened his wide fingers around the handle of her grocery cart and squeezed it, laughing, as he might affectionately squeeze her wrist.

****

Louise had to pull over on the grass to ease her car in next to a brand new Z28 parked in her drive. The car was a glossy burnt orange with tinted windows and fat, deeply-treaded tires and chrome gleaming from the wheel wells and the hood

• 103 •

scoops and the sleek, stylish lines of its body. The sun had long disappeared behind the mountains, and its coppery afterglow intensified the orange paint. Vic, who had followed her, parked his Scirroco at the curb and whistled at the car as he passed. "Ah, youth," he said to her, and he banged its fender with his fist. "All Guigintis have loot, huh?" The Camaro had the temporary cardboard plates that dealers put on new cars.

When they came around the side of the house, Andy was straddling a redwood bench under a low-hanging Spanish lantern which cast an amber glow on his chest and shoulders. He dipped his brushes in a whiskey-tinted solution and then patted them dry with paper toweling. He saw Louise. A fine blush spread web-like across his cheeks. "Dad's receptionist stopped it by," he said, standing. A set of car keys on a wide, chromium blue ring clinked to the deck, near his feet. He shook his head. "They're trying to lure me back."

She nodded, hugging the bag of groceries to her, and they both looked at each other, their gaze a third thing stuck between them. In a moment Vic coughed and she turned, remembering. She introduced the two. And Andy smiled, wiped his hand on a cloth. He leaned forward to shake with Vic, as if everything were fine. But then he was up near the house, peering through the break in the oleander. "Someone's been cruising the house for the past hour. I keep trying to see if it's mother."

Louise settled the groceries on the redwood bench and drew near, peered between the shrubs. Though it was just after dusk, and the heat of the day had flattened out, a trickle of sweat rolled down the side of her face. She swiped at it. "I'm so goddamn mad," she muttered.

Vic spread some oleander branches apart, too, and listened to their brief interchange. He whistled between clenched teeth after a moment. "Louise, I'm sorry, you're a fine-looking woman, and stuff, but—ooooo—a brand new hot rod—! I hate to tell you what I'd choose."

Andy looked blankly at him, then at Louise, and back to the street.

She took Vic by the arm. "Listen, given the circumstances, I'm going to ask that you leave."

He tightened the bola round his neck. "Now wait a minute. You promised me a *Mukfa.* And I need to find out what a Mukfa is. Sounds like something to eat!"

Louise flicked on the underwater lights, which made the pool a hole of silver brilliance shining up to the still rosy evening sky. "Ah," Vic said, the light shifting like a watery reflection on his downgazing face. She began to explain the mythical island, the boroughs of Upper Mukfa, Middle Mukfa, and Lower Mukfa, and talked about elevation, climate, cost of living, population profile. "Hah! Mutants!" Vic said, his eyes fixed on the lolling mermaids. "You know, the Alliance has been shopping around for someone to do a mural. Show some effects of nuclear holocaust. I could put in a word for you, Guiginti, if you'd like."

Andy had joined Louise by the pool. "Thanks anyway, but I'm not interested."

"Not interested? Well, you know, this latest spill was really bad. Louise can tell you all about it. Invisible radiation." He shook his head. "Why, did you know even a millicurie of californium can produce a lambent blaze? A flame-flying, heatfull fire!" His eyes leapt from Andy's to hers. "Or *pyre*," he added. "Picture the high desert as a garden of californium. You're worried about Newport Beach? Let's think about our own backyards," and he looked down at the pool. "Is that Yogi Bear?" he said. "That's better than Hanna-Barbera."

"It's"—Louise hesitated a moment—"an air traffic controller."

"An air traffic controller. How imaginative." Vic walked around the side, appraising. "I see, now. Yeah, and an airport." He bobbed his head. "Really quite good. Some extra special futuristic stuff here." He paced the perimeter of the pool, finally drawing abreast of Andy. "So, you're not a believer, is that it? You're not with us. Right?"

Andy took a step backwards from Vic. "*With* you. You mean, am I still among the living?"

Vic didn't blink. "No nukes, nuclear warfare—it doesn't get to you, huh, Guiginti?"

"I don't see that it's much different than the post WWI situation with nerve gas. We've had *it* ever since 1917 and have refrained from using it. See?"

Vic shuddered. "Yeah, but nuclear destruction—why, it's so much *cleaner!* Right, Louise? Get with me on this."

"Nerve gas was one of the cleanest tools of war," Andy told him. "Killed all the people left all the buildings."

"Well, I'm worried. Now I'm really worried. Louise, doesn't this guy worry you?"

Andy said, "The capability for total destruction has existed since long before you were born. This nuclear build-up now—it amounts to saber-rattling."

"Well, this is, I think, what he's wanting to say: Why assume that *his* generation would be tempted to pull the switch any faster than, say, *your* generation?" Louise said, parroting a thing he'd told her a half-dozen times—over breakfast, over drinks, after making love, while quarreling and in jest, in the human, feeling situations that had bound them each to the other and had carried them this far.

Vic seemed absorbed in the scene painted on the pool below him and didn't speak for a long time. "Very, very green," he murmured at last. He pointed to the sea serpent and where some of the paint had dribbled. "What an odd shape. It looks like a snake, or a dragon." Vic twisted his neck, looking at it from several angles. "But then there's that peculiar drip..." He shot a glance Andy's way and tapped his temple. "I'm thinking over what you said a while ago. Yeah. But I'm thinking you're pretty lackadaisical. Aren't you? Sit around all day, mess with these pretty colors."

"Go to hell," Andy said.

Vic rose. "You're uptight. Someone's going to jerk a knot in your tail, you walk around uptight like that. Now, I'd do it if I didn't think I'd throw my back out of commission." Then he seemed to muse. "Of course, under these circumstances your old man would probably give me a freebie. Yeah, he'd *thank* me for setting you straight."

Andy's voice was a sneer. "Let me help you decide."

He hit him in the nose, the force of which pitched Vic backward, stumbling into the oleander.

****

Out in the carport Andy was dragging a cotton car cover up over the Z28, fitting the elastic of the edges over the back bumper, tucking it in. A fine film of dusty smog had settled on the hood, a faint one, not heavy enough to dull the orange gloss. Andy looked at her as she drew near, as he continued around the car. "Did you intend to set him up?" he said. His right hand looked mummified in gauze and tape. "Or me?" He stooped down behind the car, then reappeared around the side, fiddling with some piece of chrome on the underbody.

"Probably you both," she told him. She watched as he examined the car, as he stroked the fender, rubbed at a spot there, and brushed a little dirt from it with his bandaged hand. "Are you going to keep it?"

It was as if he'd anticipated her asking. "Of course I'm not going to keep this goddamn car. It's not even a *car*," he said. "It's too many other things. It makes demands, namely that I live as they want me to live. Anything that demands *that* of you has a funny way of demanding other things, too."

In the dim light of the carport his hair had a peculiar yellow cast to it, the tiny hairs at his crown sticking stiffy straight. Her hand went instantly to her own hair but there were no tufts, only the downy, silken feel of it. "I know you're going to Stanford," she said, and always before he had hastily assured her everything to the contrary, just as her mother had said, "No, you'll never die," to her childhood fears. Now, though, he stared up into the carport.

"I'm going to go," he said, not unkindly. "That money's been there since the day I was born, it's *mine,* and I deserve it."

She closed her eyes. Her heart pounded irregularly and she saw obelisks the height of sky-scraping bank buildings tumble one atop the other, a coppery blazing cloud the size of a city engulfing them. White, hairless, naked creatures whose shattered bones jutted through the skin staggered in the streets. Wounds that would never heal—long, suppurating, running sores—gaped before her eyes. Tumors hung in flesh like sacks of oranges, and tiny ones clustered blister-like on her gums, on her lips, in her nose, pus draining as she tried to speak or flared her nostrils to breathe. She saw another such creature stumble toward her, his skeletal hands outstretched—but no love was possible. The man's penis was perennially flaccid, and the walls of her vagina had fused in an ever enduring chastity. Louise jerked her head against the vision as a horse bucking a bridle does.

"Goddamn you," she whispered. "I hope it takes you 10 years to die." And she turned her back on him, panting.

Louise heard the car before, turning, she saw it anywhere on the street, or could even determine from which direction it approached. A dark sedan cruised along, hugging close to the curb, its headlights off. The parking lights drifted like orange clouds at either end. The Cadillac seemed not to have a driver, only black there, and it slowed a bit before her driveway, catching crescents of light on its long dark hood, before shooting off down the block.

"That is so pointless," he said, watching the Cadillac glide by.

"So is this," she told him.

Andy's adam's apple bobbed. "Louise, you've got your degree, and you've got your life's focus. You forget that I don't have any of that yet. What could I ever do but fold towels at Rancho Mirage?" He let the car cover fall from his hands and stood staring at where it lay, disarranged, on the trunk. "And follow you around?"

The air was as thick as the heat. Yes, of course he made sense—but that wasn't what she wanted just now.

"What about that bike?" she asked. They both looked at the motorcycle, how it stood gleaming in the dim light, a shadowy oil spot beneath.

"The easier to come back and see you."

"A 10-hour bike ride?"

He threw his hands out. "I'm young!"

"I bought it for you," she said.

"And it'll always know the way back to you."

"But I *bought* it," she insisted.

He waited when she didn't continue and then walked around the side of the car. "Yeah, you did buy it," he said, "and it was a gift." Andy wrapped his arms around her, and because she didn't respond, he lifted her arms and fastened them around his middle for her, as if strapping something on. "We have until September. Yeah, I'll be leaving then—but I want to live. Don't let this hang like a black pall over us."

Take out a loan, buy a Corvette for him. Look for work in San Mateo County. When making love, *make him see* what he'll be leaving. She knew she'd have to contort, she'd have to twist up in every way possible—all joints, ligaments, muscles, strained to the breaking point—to get her way. Inside, her rage teemed and bubbled, ready to blow. But she knew it wouldn't. For just a flash she saw his decision as none of her business, she saw her own unhappiness as immaterial. And only after did she sense a sort of calm washing through her, welling up around a deformity, a knotted, crooked mass of tortured scar tissue that she knew as her rage.

Andy looked gloomy. "See it my way, Louise. Oh, Christ Alive, how I wish you *could!* But I can't make you. Not even when I paint your eyes," he said. She frowned, and he said, "You know, my three-breasted mermaids."

Louise smiled sadly, and they stood, arms locked about each other. "But Palo Alto," she groaned into his shoulder. "*Northern* California. It's *wet* there. They have *seasons.* Your loins will prune," she told him. "I hear they read from right to left in Northern California."

They shared a few minutes of jokes and laughter before clinging again, pressing thigh, pelvis, belly, together in the dim light. She saw September clearly: days full of that bronze sunshine; brushfires raging high in the hills; herself lying on the diving board, water rippled below, what he'd left her wavering deep down, beyond the reach of her hands, right over her head.

Princess Gilda Talks to the Unborn

In the time they'd run the Frigid Foot 10K race all up and down the banks of the Sacramento a lacy film of frost had formed on the Honda's windshield, though she'd scraped it that morning, and when they got into the car Stefan leaned back on the seat beside her, his mittened hands closed over his groin. "My balls," he said.

She looked down at the sweats he'd pulled over his nylon running shorts and nodded. "Yes," she said. She pointed to her pelvis. "My ovaries," she told him.

The engine caught and she put it in gear, began idling toward the street. Sunlight flickered across the frosted windshield, spreading a web of prismatic color.

She'd set a PR of a minute and a half over her best 10K time. In the pack of 8 minute milers she'd stayed with for the first 4 miles, some man's cranberry-colored goretex suit had swished the whole way. And then she pushed ahead in the last two miles. She surged for the 880 and for all intents and purposes sprinted the final 440, her legs stretching long in front of her, the balls of her feet, and toes, as if gripping the asphalt course. She'd raced in shorts and a sweatshirt, as had Stefan, and her own thighs had been a prickly red after, also chapped. A fine Tahatchapee was still blowing down from the nearby Sierra Nevadas. It was just too damn cold for good racing.

He leaned back, his hands a knot between his legs, the race number pinned to his shirt creasing as he moved. "Look, I've read about this happening. A guy's car broke down. In subzero weather. In Saskatchewan. He started walking through the wilderness. When he came to a town, he found a cocktail lounge, ordered a double brandy, neat, took it into the john, and bathed his balls in it. A double," he told her. He straightened out on the seat, his feet pressed hard against the floor boards. "One for each."

Dusky swerved around a couple Sunday drivers. Did he order the housebrand, she wondered, or, say, Courvoisier? "Well, I've got this beer," she said. She held out the cup she'd picked up after the race; it said "Stroh's fire-brewed" on it.

He ignored her. "That goddamn icicle 10K," he said through clenched teeth. "I could hardly lift my feet! If you can't run better than that, you may as well not run."

She kept her eyes on the road, watching the sun melt the frost, and listened to his familiar litany. "Pray to Mercury," she'd once told him, at the Firecracker Fourth of July Four-Miler. They'd just met and he was lamenting the fact that he was not a fast runner.

"You pagans," he'd murmured, laughing.

And later that morning, "You just tear the rag," he'd sputtered when early in the first mile as she overtook him and was making ready to break from the pack, she told him she saw feathers sprouting at his heels.

It was as if she could devour the road that day—feet first; she left him coughing and spitting in her wake.

"Look, I have more fast-twitch muscle fibers in my legs," was how she explained it after. The sun hung high overhead and they stood around the refreshment cabana with other sweating runners. She grabbed a couple watermelon slices and, beer in hand, moved over to a grassy area under a blooming magnolia.

He scoffed. "Well, you see, as I've had it put to me, a man can't really develop to his full potential until his late 20's. And also until he becomes a parent," he said.

She pulled at the race number still pinned to his singlet. "Name: Hollaway, Stefan. Age: Twenty-nine," she read. "You're in your prime."

He laughed and smoothed the number from her hand. "That's only part of it," he told her.

Since then she'd always beat him at any distance, something which twice monthly, when they raced, put him in high dudgeon. On the one occasion he thought he had a good chance of beating her—a rugged cross-country two-miler—she'd got her period early, cramps and anemia keeping her from attempting it.

He stood in the bedroom doorway, pulling running shorts up over his hard, tanned thighs. Jealousy got her.

"Jesus, some women runners don't even *ovulate*." A hot water bottle lay like a big red stone atop her pelvis.

"Hell, I'm disappointed too," he said. He tucked his t-shirt into his waistband with quick jabs.

She flopped back against the pillows. "No menses. No month. No moon," she said.

"Well, biology *is* destiny. At least that's what I hear." He stooped, as though he might kiss her on his way out, but bending low, instead, he touched his lips to the hot water bottle.

Her uterus went through a tight paroxysm. "Yeah, but just remember—life can't live in your body. I can give birth!" she yelled as the outer door clicked. "And that's beautiful!"

Now, in the car, Stefan was still in a brown study. "Well, that was nice and fruitless," he said.

"What?"

"Goddamn race," he told her. "I mean, runners *run,*" he was saying. "If you're not *running,* then, goddammit, you're not a runner."

He scooted forward, yanking his sweats to his knees, and stretching the leg band of his briefs aside, stared down at himself. "Oh, Holy Christ God Almighty!" he cried. "They're lead-blue!"

She glanced from the road to his groin just as he let the leg band snap back, and saw the rippled toadskin of his flesh, a faint gray color.

Stefan grabbed the dashboard. "Take me to Northpoint!" he shouted.

His clinic sat atop one of the river's palisades, at the crest of a snaky, winding road. A watertower, circa 1860, stood next to it—a national monument now, 100 meters high, this steeple of white chalky stone. She rounded the curves, climbing the cliff, and when she pulled up to the clinic, he leapt out before the wheels had stopped rolling.

A hugely glorious fountain stood before Northpoint, from which flowed two streams in opposite directions. Bridges of wide wooden planks crossed the stream and led to the front door; she watched him hurry toward the clinic, his hands shielding himself.

In the center of the fountain was a statue of a young woman. Stone water poured eternally from the urn she held. And she stood draped in ice.

It was as if she wore a shimmering ice stole.

Because the fountain had not been turned off before severe weather had set in. Thick frozen cascades appeared to spill over its sides. And fire darts shot from the ice as if from a diamond. When Dusky tilted her head, she saw lime green, orange, and turquoise flickering out over the rim of her cup. A pink mote glittered in her eye like a star.

She smiled, lifted her beer as a toast.

They were always wanting to be acknowledged.

Those dead, she thought. She sipped long and deeply from her cup.

At home, on a sidetable in her living room stood a basket in which she kept three ordinary pencils and two postcards. She'd covered the whole thing with a linen dinner napkin— because she'd heard this was one way in which to invite the Beyond to speak to her. Her Uncle Gene, the only remaining Spiritualist from Degonia Springs, had explained it. "During the war I was stationed in the Pacific. You see, I wrote to Ferd in Bakersfield every week. Now, he was my grandfather, your great-grandfather. On the Hoeppel side. He had palsy something awful. Well, after he died, mom kept a basket just like I described to you. One day there was a postcard in it for me. No one could've duplicated that unsteady script. And it was in all the colors of the rainbow! And some rainbows don't give. The *inbetween* ones. Let's say the first part of the 'B' was magenta, the curved part emerald blending to sea blue. All the letters blurred one into the other. The message went through the color wheel!" he told her.

That's what she wanted—a rainbow communication. She was being hopeful, wishing the dead would talk. It was not that in her life she experienced an absence of human voices— she wanted the *other*.

And Stefan found out.

"What is this?" he said.

She walked into the living room and found him holding what had been her childhood Easter basket in one hand, and a napkin in the other.

"Jesus," she said, "you act like a jealous husband who's found his wife's love letters."

He pulled a postcard from it, a glossy yellow one that depicted the map of South Carolina. "What gives?"

She took the postcard and turned it in her hand. The other side was as pristine and white as the day she bought it. And that's when she told him.

When she let him know she *was* different, and not just in the way most people think of themselves.

"Don't *we* talk?" he said after a few moments.

"Sure," she said. "We're talking now."

"But you want to hear the Beyond."

She smiled at the mystified expression on his face. "Well, if it has something to say, then, yes, I do want that."

He looked down at the basket, the napkin, the cards. "Is this like with fortune cookies? I mean, what do they tell you about *me?*"

She laughed. "Only the things you'd never want me to know."

He eyed her before turning to set it all back on the table. "Now, how's this go?" he said. He placed the postcards, picture side up, in the basket and draped the napkin over the entire arrangement. "Like so?" he said. "Do I need to say any words? Mutter anything?"

She stood leaning against the arched doorway, her arms crossed before her.

"Because," he said, "my father was a Mason. And I

remember how he stood memorizing their doctrine—there was procedure involved, and ceremony—muttering to himself. Oh, look!" he said, when he'd got it all in place. He leapt back from the table to admire the basket. "It's as if you're letting the postcards germinate. Or *warming* them, like hot buns." A spider plant hung just above the table; when he turned to glance back at her his hair tangled with its pale, slender leaves. "It was the Mighty Order of the Veiled Prophet of the Everlasting Light," he said. "You ever hear of it?"

She waited a moment, then took a step toward him. "Why be such a prick?" she said.

He laughed. "Well. You believe in all this."

"Yes."

His hands fell to his sides. "And I don't". They stood staring at each other, as if faced off for a fight. Time passed. Neither said anything. No sound intervened, not even a clock ticking. Then he smiled. "I'm a prick," he said. "This"—and he made a sweeping gesture with his hand to include the table—"is something I don't understand, and I'm a prick." Stefan glanced at the basket one more time, as if eyeing a third person in the room. "Yeah. Okay. Jesus," he said. "Look, want to go to that Japanese restaurant you claim I love so much?"

"Mmmmurhmmphur," she said.

"No, really."

MmmmphurHm," she told him, a little louder.

That evening, at dinner, over their miso with oysters and rice noodles, after they had sat in silence for a few moments, he said, *"Beyond* what?"

It took her a moment; she leaned back in her chair, its legs scraping on the wood floor. "Beyond a shadow of a doubt," she told him.

He stared into the broth and nodded, as if concurring with something in it. "That's nicely vague."

That next morning, Dusky got up early to get a glass of orange juice. When she passed through the living room, something seemed amiss. She stared at the basket, finally moved toward it as if magnetically drawn, lifted the napkin from it. The South Carolina card lay on top of the other, just as she'd left them. She lifted both. The other gave a view of the desert floor from the Palm Springs tramway. Mt. San Jacinto loomed in the background—glorious in its pinks and purples, like a view painted onto stage scenery, or a scrim.

She turned it over.

"Having a wonderful time. Wish you were here," it read.

In red crayon.

When she returned to the bedroom, he rolled over in the sheets. "Any messages for me?" he said.

Now, Dusky raised her beer to Northpoint's ice rainbow, and drained it, colors scattering out over the rim of the cup. What she hadn't immediately mentioned to him that morning about the other card was that it, too, had a message—and not in his hand. Powerful green strokes told her, "What is hidden will be revealed, what is revealed will be understood."

She'd held it, sunlight exploding through all the windows, everything splashed with that intense yellow light, that dry mineral light which seemed so clean, as if filtered through a white jewel, or the sections of a grapefruit.

Dusky wedged her cup between the seats and looked up to see Stefan bounding out Northpoint's double glass doors.

He had perused the Declaration of Principles of the Spiritualist Church. He had attended a message service with her, had had a reading himself, been put in touch with Princess Gilda, his guide in the spirit world. One day Dusky'd been surprised to find an area cleared off his coffee table and a breadbasket draped with a monogrammed handkerchief standing there.

A little altar, in his living room!

He told her he believed. Stefan sat, holding her hand; "D'you see? I want to be more in your life," he said, the expression on his face so serious—as if he were praying, their hands folded together, her knees touching his, the intensity of the moment hypnotic. "This isn't an 11th hour conversion," he assured her.

She liked to believe that.

He'd joined 'them'—because he hadn't been able to beat 'them.'

Now, Stefan jogged across one of the bridges, toward the car, his running shoes thundering on the wooden planks.

For just a moment he seemed to share the fountain with the ice-draped statue.

Swinging the door wide, he thudded into the passenger seat.

"You're thawed out," she observed.

"Modern medicine," he told her. "And the help of Princess Gilda," he said. "She loves me, you know."

Dusky shifted into first and began to edge away from Northpoint. "Oh, yeah? She's whispering sweet nothings in your ear?" she said. Once when she'd asked him that he'd scrunched up his shoulders: "Oooooohoooo," he'd said, "It tickles." But now he didn't smile.

"See, she knows my work here isn't finished. I mean," he told her, moving his hands in ever-expanding circles, "all my babies *aren't* frozen in me. The whole future *won't* necessarily prefer an arctic climate. My babies *aren't* sap in a frozen maple tree."

Leaning back in his seat, he sighed; he seemed to nestle into the upholstery.

"*Your* babies," she said.

Stefan winked. "They say 'Be fruitful. Multiply!'"

She adjusted the rear view mirror. Northpoint had receded, the tip of the watertower with its solid silver weathervane still visible—a spark of sunlight gleaming on it—but snuffed, as she coasted down the hill, by a stand of tall firs.

"*They*," she said.

He nodded. "That's right. Look, it's different for a man. His babies are more insistent. But, you know, all the eggs you'll ever need to produce are already in your body. They've waited ever since your birth."

When Dusky stopped for a red light, he passed his hands over her pelvis, not touching her, just moving them a couple of inches away from her body. "I enter a vibration," he said. After a moment he crossed himself. As he opened his eyes, he smiled slyly. "Princess Gilda talks to the Unborn," he said. "They say they want to return to the earth plane."

Dusky stood next to the forced-air heater in her living room, drinking a glass of pineapple juice. When Stefan rubbed his hands up her arms, she moved just beyond his reach, over to the sidetable where she set the glass down. They hadn't spoken much on the ride over.

She gripped the arm of the sofa and did a few deep knee bends, the sensation of having raced still tight in her hamstrings. She'd always enjoyed that reminder—the slight tender feeling, the *pull*—especially when she'd set a PR, but had to laugh now: the best thing about the morning was pain.

Stefan flopped down on the sofa, kicked off his shoes and socks. "Look, I don't mean to put pressure on you," he said. "It's just—Dusky, I want what I want. No one's *telling* me to have children. It's not like my boss at work is pressuring me. It's right here," he said, and he tagged his groin with his thumb.

She looked where he touched. "Oh, goddammit," she said.

After a few moments, when Dusky said nothing more, he picked up his shoes, pulled out the padded insoles, going through his post-race ritual. The small charms he kept there slid out—a tiny glass bead, a torn corner of one of the cards he'd received from Princess Gilda.

Because he'd tried the things of this world: ankle weights, shoelace weights, a vest whose compartments could hold water—for added drag. He'd alternated heavy training shoes with light racing ones.

After he'd received his first postcard from Princess Gilda, though, that had changed. "She's going to make my feet fly," he'd said. "Oh, yes, she's going to measure my courses more accurately. She'll determine my body-fat percentage!"

"Is she going to say abracadabra?" Dusky'd joked.

But he was serious. "When I'm fast," he'd say—exactly the way she, as a girl, used to say, *"When I'm grown up, when I'm an adult..."*

"Well, how fast is fast?" she asked him once.

"As fast as you," he said—no hesitation. "And a hair more. Goddamn," he said, "I want to smoke you. Oh, Christ, yes. I want to see you disappear in a rooster tail of red dust 10 yards wide," he said. He ground his fist in his palm like a pestle in a mortar.

Dusky laughed with him afterward—because it just never would happen like that.

He had the sort of gait and stride and strike that he had, and she her own. He was a flat-footed runner, landing heel first—which meant *slow.*

Yeah, biology *was* destiny, just like he'd told her.

"When I'm fast," he once said, after they'd made love and were lying in her bed, "they'll have found a cure for cancer. Peacocks might strut—tails fanned—across your front lawn." His voice dropped low. "There's a picnic in the park everyday."

She plumped her pillow and eased back against it. "What kind of sandwiches?"

He rolled over toward her. "Well, turkey and ham. And, mmmmmmmmm"—he raised his eyebrows—"cream cheese on Italian bread with black olives and pineapple slices."

Dusky's message basket stood on an antique spinet table near the corner window, sunlight glowing through the strands of cellophane Easter grass still stuck in the weave. While Stefan reassembled his shoes, she picked the basket up and stood holding it. "I wouldn't be able to run," she said.

"Honey, pregnant women run," he told her.

"Not PR's," she said, and turned her gaze on him. "You haven't even acknowledged my PR."

He tossed his shoes back to the carpet. "So, okay. Your PR. I'm happy. I'm always happy when you set a PR. But—but what if, for 9 months, I set the PR's? Could that happen?"

He held his hands out, as if he thought she might put something in them.

She looked at her fingers wrapped around the basket's straw handle, and remembered the day she'd shown him that first message, those green power strokes.

He'd nodded down at the card. "It's a man's handwriting." He rubbed his fingers across the script. "You've got a man," he said.

A moment passed.

She said, "Maybe we should introduce him to Princess Gilda." She took the card from him and stuck it to the refrigerator with the magnet that looked like a delivery box of pizza, even had strategically-placed grease stains on the lid. *"Mr. Green."*

"You're going to leave it there?" he asked.

Dusky said yeah and then went on with her life—grabbed a couple beers, opened them and poured them into tall pilsners.

He swallowed. "It's neat," he said, looking on.

But later that day—"You know," he told her, "I *like* what Mr. Green said. Check it out—*my* speed is the thing *hidden* which I'm hoping this forthcoming 10K will reveal. To me. And then I'll under*stand*," he said. "Oh, yes I will."

"What will you understand?"

They were both on their third beers, drinking them from the bottles now.

His hands swayed in the air. "Stars. Electricity. Oxygen. All the mysteries," he said. He took a long swig and wiped the foam from his lips. "Milkweed pods, for Christ's sake."

"Say what?"

"Just how do they know when to crack open and blow all that fluff around?"

Stefan had come up behind Dusky, and was rubbing the hollow between her shoulderblades. "Remember that day last month?" he whispered. "After we'd decorated the Christmas tree? What was that about? Huh?" he slid his hands over her hips and thighs, across her buttocks, as if feeling her for the first time. "You want it," he murmured into her hair. "Your body does."

Early evening. Her living room. A pink dusk luminous through slits and curtains. Nome Christmas lights throwing color all around: his knees red, nipples blue, navel and belly green. They had lain together, on the carpet, those bulbs, tangled among the tree limbs, glowing. She'd wished she could leap up and drape them about her body, slip the strands on one arm at a time, like a coat—so her skin would shimmer.

And he could see how he made her feel.

It'd be more luxurious than the thickest, silkiest mink, being wrapped in all that warm light, and the cool blues and greens.

Now, his hands moved up her ribs.

He had touched something that day, when he was going in her, he'd never touched before.

"Oh, it was good," she said.

He moaned when she said that, her words releasing him.

"Put that down," he said, tapping the basket. "Put it back now. Let me make you late this month. Let me give you that dark line here." He rubbed one finger down her belly.

The breath caught in her throat. "Okay," she said.

Stefan nuzzled her hair, kissed her neck.

After a moment, he said, "Why don't you move?"

She looked at the basket, followed its straw handle—the intertwined green and yellow and blue.

"Stefan, I love the feeling, not..."

"Shhh, shhh, now," he said, taking the basket from her. He drew the napkin back up over it, as if tucking it in. "There, now," he said—and then, "What?" he asked when he saw her expression.

"Having a baby won't make you faster."

He squared his shoulders, seemed to stand straighter. *"Faster?* How do you mean? As a runner? What's that got to do with anything? Don't change the subject, Dusky. My dreams are dreams," he told her. "I *know* that. Wait," he said. "Why're you picking that back up again?"

She pulled the napkin through the handle. The postcard of a triggerfish from the National Aquarium in D.C. lay on top; she turned it and found nothing.

"Dusky, don't look," Stefan said. "Stop doing this. Don't listen to what he has to say."

The postcard of Hussong's Cantina in Ensenada, Mexico had this written on it:

Prepare lasagne according to
Creamettes package directions.
Use all-fresh ingredients.
BUT substitute 10 artichoke
hearts for meat.
Bake at 350° 30 minutes.

She studied it.

Those green strokes, the power.

Stefan cursed Mr. Green comprehensively, naming each member of his body. His eyes jumped crazily from the Hussong's scene to her face. "I'm telling you I can't live with that guy." He stuck out his fists, knuckle-up, before her. "Mr. Green is hostile to me," he said. "Look, it's like this"—he sucked in a breath, slapping his arms against his sides—"my uncle used to brew homemade beer. And my aunt did a lot of baking."

"Oh, for Christ's sake," she cried before he'd finished, their words as in some gospel duet overlapping, her voice starting low and his trailing off.

"Just listen!" he bellowed. "I'm telling you, her bread wouldn't rise in that house, not with the beer brewing. The yeast couldn't live. The beer yeast killed it! That's the same situation with this fellow, this Green," he told her. "I can't live with him. I mean, doesn't Princess Gilda—don't you feel it toward her? Doesn't she intimidate you?"

Dusky was shaking her head. "Not if you mean, do I worry that she has a better job. More money. A nicer car. No way."

"Okay. Those things. Yes. Well, *sort* of," he said. "But *more*. Deeper."

"You're asking, am I afraid she's—she's more womanly? That her breasts are larger?"

He answered with such alacrity it stunned her. "Yes! That's it! A rudimentary intimidation. The kind that *gets* you," he said. He folded his hands between his legs, and that gesture gave birth to itself as she kept her eyes on him.

She saw him striding off into the future, his groin covered.

Dusky's chronograph chimed for 4 seconds on the hour, and his beeped twice a half minute later. She lowered herself onto the hassock, setting the basket between her feet, next to his balled-up socks and the shoes he'd kicked off. Chariots— the best running shoes made, or so he had told her the day he bought them, holding one of the gray and silver things out as if offering up to her some part of himself.

It was a heavy goddamn shoe, as stiff as a 2 by 4. She had joked around with him, though. "I can divine the future," she told him, "Let me interpret your sole." Holding it at arm's length, she'd made a show of stroking her hand over the black carbon rubber. "And, yea, there shall be 10K's," she said. "And thou shalt do amazingly well. In the final quarter mile thy feet shall pop off the pavement," she said, "and thou shalt kick thyself in the chest with thy knees."

Stefan had sat there, his fingertips, pressed together, making a little peak. "But will there be love?" he'd asked her.

She answered by flipping the shoe over her left shoulder—there was still a black smudge on the wall from where it had hit—then pulling him down to the carpet with her, as if into some new world.

Today there lay the wide expanse of room between them, so wide in her imagination, so distant, she perceived the faint horizontal curve. There were also the shoes.

She picked one up, and as if she couldn't comprehend its use, stared.

Because he could run barefoot on clouds, or wearing *Kangaroo's* feet—and he could get there sooner!—but it didn't matter a goddamn.

"Don't hold *it*," he told her. "Hold *me*. And tell me what you see."

The shoe dropped with a thud at her feet.

Dusky saw the future. Without him in it. And the future was next week.

Next week, she had an appointment with Doc Branson, to have her teeth cleaned. She had to renew car insurance. Otherwise, she still would do all the usual things. Go to the grocery—she'd probably try the artichoke lasagne. Put in some training runs. Lock her door against intruders.

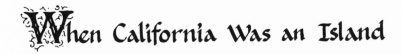

When California Was an Island

Velvet felt confused about when it was exactly that she fell in love with Griffen. When her husband left them alone in the kitchen she realized that she wasn't so much in love with Griffen then as she was with the desire to do something kind for him. Darcy had just ridiculed him. He'd stalked out of the room, laughing, clutching his head because of the hangover he'd complained about all morning, nearly gagging as he laughed—laughing, coughing, gagging at the same time—in response to Griffen's detailing a theory he'd heard—a theory he said he believed—which held that California had spent 100 years as an island. Velvet found the theory unusual but his enthusiasm charming, and she wanted to be kind. So she poured him a tall glass of the sassafrass tea she had just brewed. The sassafrass roots, thin planks all bundled together with string, planks that were a rosy, fresh, sunrise color which she imagined was at the heart of everything, were still steeping in the saucepan, and she lifted them with a fork while he watched, curious. He had never, he told her, tried sassafrass tea. By the time he finished the glass she gave him—his head tilted back while he drank so that she could see the cords of his throat smoothing up and down, the muscles there—feeling very voyeuristic as she watched the bob of his adam's apple—and by the time he set the glass down, the ice cubes clicking gently, she already knew. She knew. It was terribly intimate, her watching him drink, though she acknowledged at once that it truly wasn't at all. For Darcy poured himself a glass of sassafrass tea, and sat not two feet from her, at the kitchen table, sipping it. The whole occasion fought against any sort of intimacy. It encouraged, instead, blandness, beigeness—the way breakfast still sat about the table: bran flakes soggy in cereal bowls. And she was in fact rushing about to go to work. Velvet was forced at that moment to grab her purse, check for car keys, throw on the purple polyester blazer that she wore, flying the 20 minutes up to L.A. and the 20 minutes back down several times a day, as a flight attendant for Goldenwest. She had to brush her hair. While standing there before the hall mirror, she glanced at Griffen. She glanced at where the map he'd brought to illustrate his theory lay, now tightly rolled, on the floor near his feet, and then back to brushing. Her hair was long and brown and had bronze-colored highlights when she looked at it in a certain light. Griffen moved across the kitchen, behind her, while she stroked with the brush, and she glanced his way again. His head was turned aside somewhat but she felt certain that he had been looking at her before she shifted her eyes. He walked out of her line of vision—over by the stove, she thought; she heard him lift the saucepan—and she glanced back to the mirror, to her wrist as she snapped the brush through her hair, and then up to her face. She had never seen her eyes look more lovely. Her eyes looked lovely and she was on her way to L.A. Some days were such a waste.

By the time she got to John Wayne Airport, by the time she had checked in, greeted this flight's commuters, and climbed—stoop-backed—into the DeHavilland Twin Otter, she had hoped this feeling of wasting, of missing out, would have dissolved, become stale, a mistaken perception, nothing to concern herself with. She stood at the front of the cabin as the plane taxied, holding up seatbelts, flapping oxygen masks all over the place, talking about the unlikely event of a water landing which hardly seemed unlikely, not with the Pacific lying wide open below, and she thought about him. She thought about how one of his front teeth was jammed partially up into his gums from where he must have fallen once. It was a great, wonderful tooth that made him look so boyish. She thought about the socks he wore, even in summer, to warm his feet. They were the sort of socks people made stuffed monkey dolls out of, monkeys with those scarlet, lippy smiles that were actually heels, she'd noticed, on him. She'd overheard him tell Darcy about the flash that came bursting like surf into his sleep, and she thought about that, about how his dreams of earthquake-induced nuclear explosions were—oddly enough, she once heard him say—not unpleasant dreams, and only disturbing in the fact of their constant recurrence. Each week he said he could look forward to that flash figuring prominently in at least one dream and playing a supporting role in one or two others. He rented a bungalow on the beach at Capistrano, only a few miles from the San Onofre power plant, and this worried him. She wanted to lie with him there, to save him from his sleeping thoughts.

As she strapped herself in her seat, the awkward box of a plane jerked once and began struggling down the runway; it paused for only a moment, then—plastic panes in the windows jittery, cabin lights flickering as if shorting out, and all the ceiling panes shimmying noisily and shaking, the Otter rocked back and forth under its wings and lurched forward a long time, finally carrying them up into the sky. At that terrible moment when the landing gear lost contact with the ground and was cranked up into the wheel wells and they began to lumber up up up, she realized she did not know how to approach Griffen. He had worked with her husband so long—they were both engineers at the Fluor Corporation—she was afraid he might laugh, or feel pity for her. Both responses would trouble her equally, because she wanted to be subtle for him. She wanted to be deep for him, and cool. She wanted him to find her like that calm, quiet ocean floor divers come upon all at once after what seems miles and miles of struggling with currents and of sinking deep down. And her last thought before she moved up the the aisle to take orders for Tabs and Coors and peanuts and Chablis was a comprehension that it was too late, between her and Griffen, for precisely that sort of coolness. He'd once seen her deliver a knock-down punch—not a girlish slap, but a fist-clenched wallop—to a man in a crowded nightclub. She'd been waiting for Darcy to meet her there after work, standing up at the bar, checking her wristwatch. The punch impressed Griffen, she imagined, in a roundabout sort of way. It made him want to draw closer. He did, and this is how, in the first place, they met. He'd walked over to her, said, "It's crazy, but I feel I already know you." Her hand ached, as if bits of steel were turning slowly behind the skin, and her knuckles were puffed up and she did not much feel like dealing with another come-on. But he hadn't come on to her. He introduced himself, said he'd seen a photo of her in her husband's office, and recognized her. He sat on the stool beside her and scooped the ice from his Scotch-on-the-rocks and pressed it to her knuckles, the ice melting and dripping on their knees, but her hand held tightly between both of his, as if snugly in a glove. When Darcy showed up shortly afterward, the pain in her hand was gone, but the three of them joked all night about what she'd done to that man.

Now, she stared out the lozenge of window beside her. From the sky the Southland looked as if it had been made to be looked at from the sky: the Coast Highway traffic circle at Long Beach, for instance, was not *merely* round, no, no illusion there—but perfect and lovely, like some compass cut-out imposed on the scene. Catalina seemed adrift, shimmering in its sea mist, almost jewel-like. And that pink-gold cloud of smog which waited, as if moored, over the Southland, which you could study once you were above all the apartment complexes and their pools, some with concrete islands in their middles and palm trees on those islands, the smog that had not seemed so oppressive while you were in it, but now seeing it, breathing the oxygen-rich air in the plane, you remembered truly was—seemed almost beautiful.

She flew in that impossible pink and gold all her 5 trips to L.A. and back, sitting at the back of the cabin, gazing dazedly out the window, once not even bothering to remind commuters to fasten seat belts or put trays in upright positions or to stop smoking before landing.

That morning in the kitchen, just before Darcy burst into fits of laughter and she poured the sassafrass tea, Griffen had unfurled his map across their linoleum floor, a common map—like those United States ones hanging in schoolrooms so the children can look at purple Colorado and orange Maine and pink Alabama—one which, when she'd first answered the door to let him in, he'd wielded like a weapon—the map still rolled tightly and secured with a ribbon—resting it there against his shoulder, squinting down its long length, as if through an imaginary viewfinder, sighting her as the target.

"Pow, pow," he'd said.

And Darcy, leaning across the kitchen counter, saw him, called out some greeting—"Hey, dude" or "What's happening?" or whatever he'd said—and Velvet had let Griffen come on inside.

He joined them in the kitchen, and she'd leaned against the refrigerator, stirring her bowl of bran flakes, half-listening as they talked. Then Griffen untied the ribbon on his map to show Darcy. "Something spectacular," he told him. "Something not quite believable," he said. He unrolled and unrolled the map across the floor, hobbling on his knees as he straightened each section, hobbling sideways like a crab. The pint of Gilbey's Darcy had polished off the night before stood next to the waste can. He covered it with the map.

"I'm not so sure I want to see this," Darcy said. He sank into a kitchen chair, his feet stretched out before him.

Griffen looked up, grinning, lifted one of Darcy's feet and flattened the map below it. He said, "Don't let me bother you. Just ignore me."

But Velvet glanced up from her breakfast and didn't know how you could ignore that. It seemed the entire floor was covered with this torn, yellowed map of the States, with parts of Canada and Mexico showing at the top and bottom in orange stripes.

Griffen rested back against his heels, "There was a godawful quake," he was saying, "and then the big split. How do you think the San Andreas fault-line was created? Two shifting crusts of earth. The padres were the first to report it. They kept records and the story was passed along, like some kind of wildfire spreading up the El Camino Real." He pulled a stick of green chalk from his pocket and used it to draw a line lengthwise through the state of California, to indicate where it had split apart. "People talk about waiting for the Big One now," he said. He drew the line from Mt. Shasta through Sacramento and the Mojave all the way to where the Colorado River emptied into the blue Baja gulf. "They *talk* about waiting for the Big One," he said. "But these earthquakes now, they're just after-shocks. *Even the devastating ones*, if you can imagine. Only after-tremors, considerably diminished in size, of that first Big One. The real one."

Darcy sat there, nodding, smiling. "Oh, Griffen," he'd said. "Okay."

And he got down on the floor, too. He rerolled the map, gathering it up in quick jerks under his fingers, his wrists flicking. Griffen leaned back, smiling a little, too, as Darcy began to chuckle.

"Oh, Griffen," he'd said. And he rested one end of the half-rolled map at the root of his groin, the other end pointing upward, moving tentatively in the air, as if seeking. "It's an appendage of your paranoia," he'd said, and laughed and laughed.

After Velvet had flown home from L.A., after she'd driven the several miles from John Wayne and come through the front door, she found, spread across the living room floor, over by the tinted patio doors, her old patchwork quilt, its interlocking squares of blue and orange and purple and pink unnaturally radiant in the light filtering through the glass. A straw picnic hamper stood at one corner of the quilt, a long loaf of oddly misshapen bread extending from its partially open lid. There were two bottles of Mondavi Zinfandel, one three-quarters gone, the other, its cork lying beside it. All furniture had been pushed away from the square of quilt, as if to set it off, accentuate its separateness in the room.

Darcy was listening to "Too Drunk to Fuck"—loud—on the New Wave station, and tapping his fingers, smiling along with it because—she thought—he *recognized* it, he could see himself in some of the situations it portrayed. He was drinking from a plastic cup of wine, and she didn't know if he was drunk. The other part of it—she wasn't sure about the other part of it. They'd argued much recently; his position at Fluor had been cut to part-time—temporarily, everyone said. The news came at a point when they had to decide whether or not to refinance their condo, unable as they were to meet the three-year principle when it became due two months back.

Neither had got too near the other, as if the merest skin-touch might send them reeling, hurt, through their skinny rooms.

She set down her flight bag, and he turned.

"Surprise!" he said. He flicked off the radio.

She looked at him. He leapt off the sofa, and she accepted the cup of wine he offered.

"It's a picnic!" he said. "See?" he said. "I even cut some bougainvillea from the neighbor's fence." He pointed out the weedy, corkscrew vines, arranged to form one low bush, their tissue-like fuschia blossoms scattered about the floor.

"Well, where's my sandy beach?" she said. But she did let him lead her over toward the feast. She kicked off her shoes and stood, wiggling her toes on the hemmed edge of the quilt, heels still balanced back on the living room carpet.

She looked around. She stared out the patio doors. "I half-expected to find Griffen here—trying to persuade you, convince you."

He laughed. He began to mimic him. "Have you ever noticed how California looks like Japan? That its contours are Japan-like? Have you ever wondered if the padres noticed that?" He shook his head and unscrewed the lid of an olive jar. "The padres," he said. "Oh, God," he said, "at first I thought he meant the goddamn baseball team."

She curled her toes on the edge of the quilt, and waited for more.

"Griffen's a good time," he said. "Get this, though. Some psychic is predicting a mammoth quake late in the day on the 12th. This Friday, you know. And Griffen's thinking about it. Calculating it. Looking at his maps. Deciding in what way California might split in two. He wants us to come down for dinner that night. Have a party. Keep him company, don't you just know."

"Well, that sounds nice," Velvet said. "It sounds like a good idea."

He stared up at her through the fringe of his bangs. "Uh-uh," he said. "Fluor's got me down in Tijuana that afternoon. Those fuckers," he said, and he sighed. "They've got me presenting designs for oil rigs off Baja."

"Oh," was all she said.

He rolled a slice of provolone and ate part of it. "But you go," he said. "I can drive up from Tijuana in two hours. I won't make it for dinner, but I'll be there."

Velvet thought about how experts were always predicting the quakes, how nothing ever came of those predictions. Once, on a day when no one had predicted anything, she'd sat in a Taco de Carlos, half-way through the quesadilla she'd ordered, and watched the hanging plants in the window jiggle. "It's a earthquake! *A* earthquake," some kids in the parking lot shouted. They were playing and having a good time, wadding up their taco wrappers and hurling them like hand-grenades at each other.

"Well, I've got to say I liked what Griffen said. I believed it." She waited. "I wish you'd tell me stories like that."

"I tell you stories," Darcy said. "I tell you stories all the time. Like the one about the boy and girl. How the boy bought the avocado 3 days ago and ripened it in a paper bag so that he could strip, slice, and chop it for the salad." He indicated a wooden bowl, shadowy with greenery. "About how the boy made the bread with his own hands—almost killing the yeast in the process—and then dragged the neighbor's weeds in through the patio door. And how the girl still stands there before him, as if on ceremony, as if uninvited—she hasn't even sat down on the picnic quilt yet—thinking, talking about other things. I tell you those stories," he said. He took a long draught from his wine, watching her, first, over the rim of the cup, then tilting his head back, his eyes smoky and huge as he peered at her through the plastic.

"You haven't even asked me about L.A.," she said.

He spread his arms before him. "I did this *because* of L.A. Because I wanted to do something, something fun. Because I knew you'd be up in that old stringbag Goldenwest calls a plane all day. O, L.A.," he said. "L.A. uber alles. Is it still there? Does it still smell like burnt toast and garbage?"

She nodded. She said, "I called Coldwell Banker while I was up there."

He riffled his hands through his hair. "Okay," he said. "Well, okay." He looked at her. "I know we've got to decide about that. We can wrap one mortgage around another—get creative about it—wrap and wrap and wrap until it hugs tight, strangling. Or we can let it all go. We've got to decide about that," he told her, "but not now. This is a night all about being able to ignore those things, right? Can we do that?" He dropped his hands to his thighs with a slap and stared at the food around him. "Anymore, I feel like I'm on vacation here. Really. I'm not living, not at home." He looked up at the walls of their condo. Neither incarcerated, nor permanent," he said—"you know, Just Visiting, like on the Monopoly board. Let's live it up."

He fished an olive from the jar and popped it in his mouth.

"So you wanted me to ask about L.A.," he told her, "and I've asked about L.A. Now, come on," he said. He took her hands in his and pulled her clumsily down to the quilt. He leaned near to kiss her, and when his lips touched hers, she felt him press just the tip of his tongue between them, rolling the olive from his mouth to hers.

He smiled at her surprise.

He said, "This is that sandy beach as far as I'm concerned."

On Friday, Velvet drove the 30 miles to Griffen's amid tight, tentative traffic and the bad Santa Anas that had blown in from the desert. They swirled about her car and rocked it as she tried to drive steady on the freeway. They were frustrating. She kept expecting them to blow up a storm, but they never ever did do that. She did not know how a place could have a particular natural disaster on one day—say, a Wednesday— and a completely different one on a Thursday. Saturday might threaten creative financing, Sunday an earthquake— one an unnatural thing, the other natural? Or perhaps too alike, she thought, each concerning pieces—no matter how small, large, or shifting—of real estate.

She fought with the steering to keep the car on the road, and concentrated on Griffen. He had junk—old sundials with metallic-colored glass globes, iron works of art—displayed in the yard around his bungalow. She liked the ten pink plastic flamingoes he had stuck in the sand and ice plants in his backyard—it looked as if they were grazing. Little of the junk was in his house, though. There, he had second hand furniture. Good Oriental rugs covered the floors. Next to the china hutch stood a female mannikin he'd picked up at a JC Penny that was going out of business. He'd sprayed the mannikin gold, and in the summer she wore only the frilly, fluffy part of a pink tutu at her hips. In the winter, he dressed her in a wide batik scarf, as a kind of wraparound skirt, the tutu lying like a powder puff at her ankles, as if anxious again for summer. Her name was Stella.

Brushfires had started in the canyons, and the Santa Anas only made them worse. Great gusts of smoke and flying ash billowed up out of the hills. When Velvet stopped at Signal Liquor for wine and came back out, she found her car dusted with a powdery cinder, as if several people had smoked cigarettes while standing there and had tapped their ashes on it.

When she pulled up in Griffen's drive she saw the banner he had slung across his front porch. It read "Merry Big One

Day" and flapped frantically in the wind. She ducked under it as she approached the door.

He'd fixed a simple sit-down meal. The swordfish baked in the oven, and he brought salads over to the table.

"Nice," Velvet said. She admired the single candle in its pewter candlestick.

"Isn't it?" he said. "I feel a little domestic."

"Women could get ideas," she said—"the kind of treatment they receive in your home." She reached for the French.

Griffen straightened a napkin on her lap and sat across from her. "No," he said. "No, they never do."

She said, "You *need* a woman to get ideas." She concentrated on bringing a bit of spinach and avocado to her lips. "Someone carefree. And fun. Someone like me, for instance."

He chewed a moment and smiled. "Oh, someone like you'd never have me."

"No?"

He reached for the French. "And even if she would, she'd realize soon after she had got home and cut all the price tags from me and taken me out of my box to play that I truly wasn't what she'd wanted in the first place."

"Having kept the sales slip," she said, "she could then return you."

He laughed and chewed. "Well, I *don't* think of us in that way."

"What happens when you try?"

"Oh, I think of Darcy approaching me, madly, wielding a Louisville Slugger. As would be his right," he said. He leaned back, staring up at the wall. It seemed he saw it all vividly there. "It's comical," he said. "Like some wild burlesque. You see the end coming a long way off."

"Whom do you think of in that way?" she asked him several silent moments later in which she had not lifted her fork.

He appeared surprised. "Why, no one." He leaned in. "Velvet, I've got that island to think of. Poor California. I'm obsessed, I tell you." He fit a wedge of tomato in his mouth.

"So there's no one?"

He thought about it. "No," he said. "Well, wait," he said. "No, I don't know." He frowned at her. "What do you mean?"

Velvet looked at her elbows, both balanced on the table on either side of her plate, and her hands cupped, the fingers curled gently in. She was once privy—indirectly, through Darcy—to Griffen's careful courtship of a blonde technician

with whom he worked. She was privy to the bunches of flow-
ers he sent this woman, privy to the dinner reservations he
made in exotic and special restaurants—even flying out to
Palm Springs once, just for the evening. But this courtship
had gone only so far, and then no farther. Far enough, Velvet
had thought at the time, just to begin to get interesting; not
far enough, she'd felt certain, for the magic to have worn off.

Now, he leaned back in his chair and said, "Stella."

She smiled.

"I dream of Stella," he told her, closing his eyes. "Cone-
shaped breasts," he said. "That smooth shadow between the
legs." He grinned at her and picked up his fork.

She turned to the plate before her, the trashy remains of
salad there. She smelled the swordfish baking and didn't feel
up to the rest of the meal.

"Where are you going?" he asked.

She punched on the TV and flopped back against the
couch. "I'm wondering about Darcy," she said. She turned an
olive pit on her tongue and watched as, there on the screen,
Vince Ferragamo let fly a Hail Mary pass. A ribbon of words
slid by at the bottom of the picture, updating various brush-
fires in the area. "I'm worried about him," she said.

She heard Griffen's bare feet on the kitchen linoleum, that
slapping, squeaking sound. She heard the clatter of the broil-
ing pan, then his chinking about in the dinnerware. She
stared at his softball trophies on top of the TV—all gold men
winding up to pitch balls. She stared at the antique lead
figurines there, too, which he collected, figurines he occa-
sionally picked up and studied with such exquisite concentra-
tion on his face. Lots of things in his house reminded her of
fun the three of them had had together. There was a Gumby
clinging to the TV antenna which she and Darcy had sur-
prised him with after he told them he enjoyed watching old
Gumby reruns each morning on Kids Karnival. He had an
aquarium with nudibranchs and sea cucumbers—ugly, tube-
like invertebrates—and one triggerfish that swam about,
lonely, between decorative chunks of glass. The tank, its bub-
bling water action, reminded her of the time, the winter
before, up at Point Reyes with Griffen and Darcy—an unset-
tling memory. She closed her eyes and saw circles of ice wheel-
ing about them, smashing against the rocks, and her and
Griffen swimming, like fools, in torn wetsuits among the
tidepools while up above, on a low cliff, Darcy crouched,
watching. Her limbs had gone prickly numb in the icy water,
and she had felt the waves sucking at her, trying to pull her

along with them—and too persuasively, for all at once she had wanted to go with them, the water like salt pure and wet at her mouth. But Griffen had charged her, his thick, broad shoulders rising out of the water. He herded her up against the rocks, swam her into a corner there. And clinging to a ledge-like overhang as she gulped water and tried to catch her breath, he had laughed at her. He'd snapped his head back, laughing soundlessly but so hard his body shook, agitating the water around them, and tears spilled from his eyes, rolled into his sideburns. Then, "Look," he had said. He had pointed out the anemones carpeting the rock there behind her, their scarlet tentacles waving like grass, the tiny crabs dashing sideways, suspiciously, from one pool to another. "Ohhhhhhhh, look," he'd said, his finger retiring from an advancing crab.

When Velvet opened her eyes Griffen was sitting before her on the hassock, his knees clamped together and a plate balanced on top of them. The silverware flashed as he cut bites of fish for her. He had brought the candle from the dinner table over to cheer her. It flickered wildly on the arm of the sofa.

"Come on, Velvet. Merry Big One Day," he told her. He lifted a buttery chunk of fish to her lips.

"This is stupid," she said. She opened for the meat and chewed. "Who's merry here?"

The TV showed a head-shot of Georgia Frontiere cheering wildly.

Griffen had laughed at Point Reyes as if to scold Velvet—and also out of some enormous relief.

While clearing the table, cleaning up the kitchen mess, Velvet and Griffen finished the bottle of wine she had brought, and he opened another. He got out some maps—one a ragged parchment thing—and he talked about it, California as an island. He even had one of those tacky tourist postcards which showed giant oranges sprouting from Southern California and luscious men and women diving—bent at the waist—as if off the very tip-edge of the coast, aiming far out into the Pacific. He'd cut the state in two, along much the same jagged line he'd drawn on the map he'd brought to their condo, and showed her what the pieces looked like apart, and how they could be fitted exactly back together again. His cheeks were flushed—whether from the wine or his enthusiasm, she wasn't certain—but she liked imagining what he explained: set adrift, the state separated. He was cutting a postcard up for her to keep as her very own when the phone rang.

He got up to answer it, and she sat there, handling the pieces.

"You're drunk," she heard him say in the hallway. "Okay, okay," he said; then, "Here," and he leaned around the corner, holding the phone out to Velvet.

She looked down at the mess of maps before her. She took the receiver from him and pressed it against her ear. Darcy told her he was still across the border, that Fluor was jacking him around, that he didn't think he'd be able to get away before midnight. "Just wait for me there," he said. "I mean, from what I hear, fires are skipping across the freeways. Everything's burning. They've shut down the northbound 405. You're safer there," he told her.

But Velvet had to strain to hear him. His voice kept going under static, she kept losing him.

"Look," he said, "we'd be lucky if our condo had burned to the ground by morning. But stay," he said, "and wait. Just make Griffen put up with you for a while. He's got room, and I'll swing by as soon as I can manage it."

Velvet hung up the phone and told Griffen what Darcy had said.

"Well, don't worry about him. He'll arrive. We can wait for him." He glanced back to the maps on the table. "Come on. I've got to show you what happened to the L.A. Basin when California was an island. And also the Salton Sea. It's how it was formed. At least that's my theory."

They returned to the table and she watched his wide hands as he touched the maps, as he traced the skinny lines so that she had to bend close, following his finger, to see. She finished her glass of wine and he refilled it. After a while the lines began to blur, to swim, to blend back together, as if woven.

Velvet looked at her watch. It was well after midnight. "It's over," she said. "Waiting for the Big One." She held her wrist out so he could read the time.

He leaned back, didn't sigh as she thought he might.

"Well, you can't be too certain," he said. "Though really all day I've been waiting for the lampshades to begin wiggling. I've been waiting for things to move of their own accord. I've looked for some tremor to send Stella tottering across the room."

She smiled at that, and glanced at Stella, noticed the scarf at her hips, the fluff of tutu at her feet. She expected Darcy to come exploding through the door at any moment. She didn't want to stay, didn't want to wait. But aside from the 405 freeway there was only one other way to go north—up Coast Highway. And it had all those traffic circles, with all those stop lights. It was late and Velvet didn't much feel like stopping.

Griffen began rolling his maps.

"Listen, Darcy will get here. It'll be all right. Okay?"

She nodded. She watched as he tied ribbon around the maps and placed them on the table.

They sat like that for several moments; then, suppressing a yawn with a smile, Griffen shook his head. "I think I better lie down. The wine, you know. We'll still be waiting, though."

Velvet stood when he stood. He had a sofa bed in the living room, but he offered her his bed—a humongous king-sized one, a veritable wilderness of sheets, a bed you could get lost in. He steered her down the dark hallway to the room. "And when he gets here—even if it's 3 or 4 in the morning— we're going to get up and have a party. Right?" he said.

He rummaged about in the bureau drawer and tossed her a pair of pajamas. They were large—his size—and made of a soft flannel material, with fuzzy-looking stripes and horizontal lines of green and blue interlaced in the fabric. He left her there on the edge of his bed as she kicked off her shoes, began removing her socks.

She tossed her clothes on a chair, slipped his pajama top on, flicked off the light. Velvet got into bed and lay first on her side, then she rolled over on her back and stared up at the ceiling. When Griffen lay his body down here—and she wondered which side of the bed he preferred—he saw nuclear explosions. "Imagine one blinding flash," she'd heard him say once, "and a dense cloud of red bubbling up there." He'd fluttered his hands, then—the fingers curled gently in. "Bubbling up there like boiling tomato soup. Bubbling higher than you can stand to look without losing balance. Boom, boom, boom, boom." This was where she wished to lie, her body against his, around his, on his, as if to protect, as if she could do that.

She watched starlight cut through a crack in the venetian blinds. It seemed to change each time she opened her eyes— sometimes resting half on the carpet, half on the closet door, other times slicing a straight path along the wall. After a while, a while in which she heard the house grow still, only the wind whistling at the windows, the light slashed across the foot of the bed.

Velvet got up and headed for the bathroom. She splashed water on her face and examined the smeared mascara ovals beneath her eyes, then turned off the light.

She had stood in the living room doorway a long time, letting her eyes adjust. The TV seemed to emerge from the darkness, also Griffen's softball trophies—she saw the gleaming contours of those men, those men ready to let the ball leave their fingers—and listened to the bubbling hum of the aquarium, the water itself creating a shifting light.

She heard the groan of springs from the fold-out sofa and saw Griffen lift up on one elbow, looking her way.

He sat up a bit, the sheets creating deep shadows around his hips, between his legs. She stood until she felt the muscles in her thighs go hard and heavy. Then she moved toward the sofa, sat on the mattress beside him, feeling it shift her way as she did. She rubbed his hand through the covers, the fabric slipping between his fingers.

"What if he comes in?" Griffen said.

But she didn't stop. She lay back against the pillows, and after a moment slipped under the covers. The aquarium hummed. Objects in the room—TV, trophies, Stella in her corner—seemed somewhat cloaked in shadows. Velvet placed her hand on the back of his, feeling the bones and knotty veins there, and like a child playing with a toy car, slid it across her hip, up her ribs; she guided his hand to her breast and held it there. She felt terribly shy at that moment.

He seemed to smile, which didn't make any of it easier. He smiled—she was afraid he might giggle. She felt embarassed, confused. She felt Cromagnon. Had she simply jabbed a finger at her breast and grunted in order to make him understand she wanted him to touch her there she could not have been more obvious. There she was. Not a subtle thing about her.

But Griffen rubbed his fingers across her breast, teasing the nipple; it popped erect immediately, like a hard little button.

He leaned away from her, still touching her. His eyes seemed so deep in his tanned face. They seemed to know at once all she was about. The look he gave her, while sweet and serene, said, I did that more for your benefit than mine. She waited, unsure of what to do with that look. She thought of jamming her knee up into his groin. Or bringing her hand around from where it was now hooked under his waistband and slipping it down, gently, to cup him. Slipping it down in a joky way so he could understand she recognized the silliness they were engaged in.

She did slide her hand around. She stroked him through his shorts, the roomy cotton fabric wrapping partially around his cock, like a kitchen towel or pot-holder around the handle of a too-hot pan.

He giggled at that point.

And so did she. She felt for the first time they understood each other.

When she moved to pull his shorts away from his hips, though, he stopped her. He held her hands. "Wait a minute, now," he told her. He pressed against her, his eyes big. He was smiling.

The wildness in his chest reverberated there in her own.

Then he slid his hands up her hips, across her belly, along her ribs. He pulled the placket front of her pajama-top away and held it out like that, as if in the moment he held it he could choose either to ball it up tightly in his fist—to yank it—or , instead, to undo the buttons. He began to undo the buttons.

"Are you awake?" she asked.

His arm lay partly across her brow, and he lifted it to look at her. She shrugged down lower in the sheets, sliding against him, for warmth. "Good morning," she said.

Griffen turned from her to the window, which seemed only a pale gray page in the wall. "Yeah?" he said. "It's a good morning? We're still attached? Not floating around?"

They got up and began refolding the bed. It clanked and moaned as they clamped it back together, and then slid easily down into the sofa. They arranged the cushions on it. The room looked as if a bed had never been there in the first place, except there were the small indentations in the carpet, from where its legs had stood, all that pressure.

He seated her on the sofa, taking her hands in his, as you would for a child, and turned the TV set on.

It was Kids Karnival.

She watched Gumby and Pokey melt and bend and stretch and curl and roll themselves into bouncy balls while he busied himself in the kitchen with the waffle iron. Velvet glanced at the aquarium, the triggerfish lumbering like a cloud between chunks of glass, casting a pencil-like shadow on the bottom with its long, slender body. It was just waking up, just getting its color back. Griffen had laughed last night as he had that time at Point Reyes, his eyes glittery, tears leaking from the corners. After trying for several minutes he had rolled from her, his body shaking with silent laughter.

Velvet ate breakfast, then walked down to the beach, sitting for a while, first with only her toes touching the froth and water that rushed in, then her entire feet as the tide began to rise. She sat, sand melting away underneath her.

Some pipers scurried about, feeding off the tiny goodies the tide left behind. Velvet couldn't see that the tide left anything, but the birds stuck their beaks in the sand nevertheless, making little pocks there, and scampered on their twiggy, backward-jointed legs—moving quickly, like a cartoon parody of hurry—as the tide rushed back. She'd been sitting like that, watching, when she heard someone behind her.

It was Darcy.

He stumbled amid the ice plants at the crest of the beach, kicking sand up in little clouds with his flip-flops. "Tijuana!" he yelled, and he stopped. His arms were full of things—she saw one of Griffen's pink plastic flamingoes, some folded paper roses. He resituated them and moved toward her. "Teee-ahh Wahh-nah," he said. "Yeah, good old Aunt Jane's doing fine." He dropped a plastic bag full of pistachios at her feet and a pack of cigarettes on top of it. They were donkey shit cigarettes.

His breath was beery as he leaned to kiss her.

He said, "I was up all night and this is what's left of it." He pulled two Dos Equis from his windbreaker and popped the top on one. He handed it to her and she watched its foamy head rise around the opening. The can was wet in her hands.

He opened one for himself.

"You look goddamn silly," she said. She pointed to the floppy sombrero he wore squashed low over his face.

"Well, I feel goddamn silly," he said. "And I'm sorry to have missed Griffen's vigil. Though here's what I think. I think it happened." He took a sip from his beer and watched a fishing trawler heading out to sea.

Velvet followed it with her eyes, too. The tide had established a rhythm of three crashing waves that truly shook the ground beneath them—the way thunder sometimes can—then the waves flattened completely, fell still and glassy, seemed more like those on the quiet surface of a lake for several seconds.

Darcy said, "Yeah, the state split its seam last night—say,

at some wee hour—and then came back together again—neat—as if glued at the edges. *I* felt it. I *know* it to be so. I'm telling you the earth shifted under my feet."

She smiled.

He reached into the plastic bag and drew out a handful of pistachios, began cracking them, eating the meat, and tossing the shells in the sand, which confused the pipers and gulls who flocked about, hungry. "Here's the thing," he said, "I got up early, drove to the border, told them I was an American citizen, and crossed over. Everything was still smoking in San Diego—all the hills—but I felt *free*. Fuck Fluor. Fuck that condo, too. We're getting out of there."

"Well, we'll have to," Velvet said, "if we don't carry through with the papers."

"No, Velvet. We *want* to get out. See it *that* way. It makes all the difference."

She sifted sand back and forth between her hands, sifting out all the tiny shells. A garland of kelp washed up between her knees but she didn't reach for it. Darcy said, "Frankly I hope the place shattered right down the middle. I hope it's lying destroyed when we get back. Two-by-fours jutting out in all directions, glass splinters, stucco, the tile roof just one avalanche of red dust on the sidewalk."

His fingertips were stained scarlet from handling the pistachio shells, prying them apart, and she looked at them, at the way the dye had sunk deep in his fingerprints. At breakfast Griffen had sat on the kitchen chair next to hers, a filmy speck of blackberry jam on his chin which he didn't know was there. He had made perfect waffles—golden on the surface and soft inside, almost creamy, the jam melting deliciously and sinking down, forming syrupy pools in the grid of square holes. He said he wanted to make love to her. "Last night"—it was because he'd been drinking, that was the problem, things could be so different. "You've got to promise me a raincheck," he said. She wanted to believe what he told her.

His fingers trembled as he lifted his mug of coffee.

And she'd said yes. It took her only a second to think about it. It was what she'd wanted, what she'd felt herself moving toward since first pouring the sassafrass tea.

He seemed to sigh. He pulled her to him, his chin resting delicately at her hairline, her cheek pressed to the soft skin of his throat. He barely breathed. She thought he might kiss her. He held her, completely still.

The moment stunned her.

When he drew back to smile, a strand of her hair stuck to the jam on his chin.

Now, Darcy clapped his hands together and rubbed them through the sand. "I'm going to tell him," he said. He stood and gazed woozily back toward the house. "I'm going to tell Griffen he missed out. Tell him about how things started shaking down in the Baja." ·

She watched as he walked away, the flamingo clamped under his arm. He grew very small, seemed to become the only thing on the beach, something moving away from her, and she wondered. She had got what she'd wanted many times in the past, but now—for the life of her—she could not remember what those things had been like.

The waves boiled up around her, peaked, and dissolved. She listened to the conch-shell sound of it.